THE
LIFE AND TIMES OF LEWIS WETZEL

The
Life and Times
of
Lewis Wetzel

(Revised and Second Edition)

By C. B. ALLMAN

*Assistant County Superintendent of Marshall County
Schools, Moundsville, West Virginia*

ILLUSTRATED

Press of

E. V. PUBLISHING HOUSE

Nappanee, Indiana

Facsimile Reprint Published 1995 by

HERITAGE BOOKS, INC.
1540-E Pointer Ridge Place,
Bowie, Maryland 20716
(301) 390-7709

ISBN 0-7884-0204-8

A Complete Catalog Listing Hundreds of Titles
on Genealogy, History, and Americana
Available Free on Request

THE LIFE AND TIMES OF LEWIS WETZEL

PRINTED IN THE UNITED STATES OF AMERICA

THIS BOOK

IS

REVERENTLY

DEDICATED

TO

GEORGE W. BOWERS

PREFACE

IN this work the author has consulted original records that could be obtained, and made use of the traditions handed down from generation to generation that could be verified. He has derived considerable aid from former writers on the Wetzel family, and drawn on a large acquaintance among the Wetzel descendants.

This narrative is true in so far as records, written and oral can be found on the subject. The story is not intended to praise or condemn Lewis Wetzel but to picture him as he was, a hero of the frontier of his day. The writer is indebted to the State Historical Society of Wisconsin for permission to use the Draper Collection of Manuscripts from Lewis Bonnett and others concerning this narrative; also Cecil B. Hartley's, *"Life of Lewis Wetzel,"* R. C. V. Myer's, *"Wetzel The Scout"*, Alexander Scott Wither's, *"Chronicles of Border Warfare"*, Dr. Alfred P. James, of The University of Pittsburgh, Wills DeHass, *"History of Indian Wars"*, Charles McKnight, *"Our Western Border"*, Ex-Senator George W. Bowers, of Mannington, West Virginia, President of the Wetzel-Bonnett Reunion, and Annie A. Nunns, Assistant Superintendent of the State Historical Society of Wisconsin, Madison, Wisconsin. He wishes to acknowledge the assistance of Scott Powell, author of the *History of Marshall County*, Eli Huggins, 92-year old Civil War Veteran and a descendant of Martin Wetzel, M. C. Gilpin, Assistant Editor of the Pennsylvania Farmer at Pittsburgh, Pennsylvania, J. T. McCreary of McCreary Ridge, Marshall County, West Va., The Marshall County Historical Society, Frank O. Good of Martinsville, Indiana, Elizabeth M. Fletcher of Martinsville, Indiana, Dr. C. H. Ambler of West Virginia Uni-

versity, Morgantown, W. Va., and all others who assisted
in any way with the work.

It has been a great pleasure to gather the material necessary in writing this book. May this great country of ours
ever remember the work of this famous pioneer, of his family, and of his friends in helping blaze the westward trail
of civilization.

I thank all who helped in any way with this work.

Very truly yours,

C. B. ALLMAN

TABLE OF CONTENTS

LIST OF ILLUSTRATIONS

THE
LIFE AND TIMES OF LEWIS WETZEL

CHAPTER I

INTRODUCTION

HUNTER of red men, hunted by both red and white, condemned murderer, avenger, untamed adventurer, protector of his race, bold frontiersman of unerring aim and bashful fiddle player in whose company only children and dogs delighted, Lewis Wetzel stalks the pages of early Kentucky, Pennsylvania, West Virginia and Ohio history as a half myth whose exploits have thrilled fireside circles for generations.

Measured in standards of to-day he was an outlaw and trouble-maker; measured in the standards of his day he was a hero and the champion of outraged humanity. Perhaps an account of his adventures may give us an insight into the trials and terrors of pioneer times, the fears and cruelty, the hardships and hopes of the settler, the crude justice, blind passions and dogged determination which made up the sharp and high-tempered edge of civilization that pushed back the forest and the Indian to make room for the Whites.

Lewis' father, "an honest Dutchman" named John Wetzel, was no Indian fighter, but his five sons spent most of their lives seeking Indian scalps or hustling to save their own.

Martin Wetzel, brother of John Wetzel, was born in 1731, in Holland.[1] John Wetzel, father of Lewis Wetzel, was born in 1733 in Holland.[2] The Wetzel family moved to Switzerland about 1740. In 1747 they came from Switzerland to Pennsylvania. Their mother died on board the vessel a few days after they were at sea, and upon landing at Philadelphia they were deserted by their stepfather. Martin aged 16 and John aged 14 were sold for their passage.

Martin located afterward in Oley Township, Berks County, Pennsylvania, and John located in Hereford Township, Pennsylvania. where they resided until about 1756.[3] Martin resided on a farm, which he owned and left to his descendants. He served in the Revolutionary War and participated in the battles of Long Island, Brandywine, and Germantown. He was a man of good judgment, of strict integrity, and honor. He married a Miss Bertolet, about 1772, of Oley Township, daughter of one of the Huguenot

---

1. *Thirty Thousand Names of Emigrants*, by Rupp, page 121, says that John, Martin and Heinrich Wetzel came to America Sept. 16, 1747, on the Palatine Imported in Queen Elizabeth's Hope from Rotterdam east from Deal, England, with 300 other emigrants.

H. S. Whetsell, editor of *"The Preston County Journal,"* at Kingwood, W. Va., says that Hans Martin Wetzel came to America in 1731; Johan Jacob in 1734; Johan Werner in 1738; Jacob in 1746; Hans George in 1750, and Johannis in 1754. It was Johan Jacob or Jacob Werner that was the father of Captain John Wetzel who married Mary Bonnett, daughter of Captain John Bonnett, Sr.; also Martin and Heinrich Wetzel. It is not known if the six Wetzel's were brothers or not as some of them came from the Rhine River of Germany. "Wetzel" is German. "Whetsell" is the English way.

2. Bonnett to Draper, *Draper's Mss.* 2E8 in State Historical Society of Wisconsin, Madison, Wisconsin.

3. Pennsyvlania Archives, Volume 18.

settlers of Berks County. We have no further record of her. They had one child, Abraham, born November 15, 1773, in Oley Township, Berks County, Pennsylvania, who died on July 9, 1846, in Harrisburg and was buried there. He was twice married. First to a Miss Deffebaugh, and had an issue, and secondly, August 2, 1810, by Rev. F. D. Peterson, to Mary Reynard, daughter of Henry and Elizabeth Reynard, born May 16, 1786, died February 16, 1860, leaving the following children: Elizabeth, Martin and Mary. Martin, Sr., died in 1822 and was buried in the cemetery of Zion's Lutheran Church, on Fourth and Chestnut Streets, Harrisburg, Pennsylvania.

John Wetzel and Mary Bonnett were married in 1756 and the couple moved to Rockingham County, Virginia, where they lived for a few years until they moved to Lancaster County, Pennsylvania. Of their children Martin was born in Rockingham County, Virginia, and Lewis Wetzel[4] was born in Lancaster County, Pennsylvania.

The Wetzel Family

The children of Captain John Wetzel, Sr., and Mary Bonnett Wetzel were: Martin, born 1757; Christiana, born 1759; George, born 1761; Lewis, born August, 1763; Jacob, born September 16, 1765; Susannah, born 1767; John, Jr., born 1770.[5]

Martin Wetzel married Mary Coffielt, now called Coffield,[5] in 1784 or 1785. Their children were three sons and eight daughters: George, born 1785; John, born February 6, 1797; died February 2, 1879, having married Elizabeth Miller, July 19, 1825, with Henry Furlong performing the

---

4. Lewis Wetzel was my great uncle, my grandfather's mother being Sarah Wetzel, a daughter of Jacob Wetzel, one of Lewis' younger brothers. The name Wetzel was first applied to a person who whetted, whittled or sharpened tools with a cutting edge.

5. Lewis Bonnett to Lyman C. Draper, *Draper's Mss. 20S64, and 20S48*, in the State Historical Society of Wisconsin, Madison, Wisconsin.

ceremony.[6] The children of John and Elizabeth Miller
Wetzel were: Martin, born August 16, 1834; died July 18,
1904; Lewis; John T.; Hiram; William, and Nancy. Martin
married Margaret Haynes. John T. married Mary Purdy.
The family of Lewis' wife is unknown. Similarly, the family of Hiram's wife is not known, but her given name was
Rosa, and the same is true of William's wife whose given
name was Helen. Nancy Wetzel married George Crow.
John Wetzel's wife, Elizabeth Miller Wetzel, was born in
1803; died October 2, 1848.[7]

Martin and Mary Coffield Wetzel's son Lewis, married,
but we know nothing of his wife's family except that her
given name was Margaret.

Martin and Mary Coffield Wetzel's daughter Sarah, who
was born in 1783, married James McCreary, September 11,
1803.[8] She died November 30, 1848. James McCreary was
born in 1775 and died March 17, 1817.

Martin and Mary Coffield Wetzel's daughters, Polly,
Barbary, and Catherine, never married. Barbary was born
February 16, 1792, and died December 31, 1863. Catherine
died young. Chloe Wetzel, also called Clarissa, daughter
of Martin and Mary Coffield Wetzel, married Ezekiel Caldwell; Rhumana, also called Rhuie and Ruth Wetzel, daughter of Martin and Mary Coffield Wetzel, married Alexander
Caldwell.[9] Ruth Wetzel Caldwell was born 1794, and died
February 26, 1865. Alexander Caldwell was born August
4, 1798, and died June 25, 1888. Rhoda Wetzel, daughter

6. *Marriage License Book 1*, found in the Clerk of the County
Court's Office in the Courthouse at Wheeling, Ohio County, West
Virginia.
7. The family are buried in the Blair's Ridge cemetery, two
miles off U. S. 250 in Marshall County, West Virginia.
8. *Marriage License Book 1*, p. 90, found in the Clerk of the
County Court's Office, of Ohio County, in the Courthouse at Wheeling,
West Virginia. Mary Coffield Wetzel, wife of Martin Wetzel, died at
Martin Wetzel's old home place on Wheeling Creek in 1836 or 1837.
Bonnett to Draper, *Draper's Mss. 24S48*, in State Historical So-
ciety of Wisconsin, Madison, Wisconsin.
9. *Marriage License Book 1*, found in the Clerk of the County
Court's Office, in the Courthouse at Wheeling, West Virginia.

of Martin and Mary Coffield Wetzel, married Hamilton Gosney December 4, 1827, with Thomas Dakan performing the ceremony.[10] Peggy Wetzel, daughter of Martin and Mary Coffield Wetzel, married Jacob Daten. Martin Wetzel died in October, 1829, at the old Wetzel homestead on Big Wheeling Creek.[11] His daughter, Mary (Polly) Wetzel, died May 6, 1846, at the old homestead on Big Wheeling Creek.[12]

Christiana Wetzel, daughter of John and Mary Bonnett Wetzel, married Jacob Wolf;[13] they had one son, John Wolf.[14]

George Wetzel and the famous Lewis Wetzel, sons of John and Mary Bonnett Wetzel, never married.

Jacob Wetzel, son of John and Mary Bonnett Wetzel, married Ruhama Shepherd, daughter of William Shepherd, niece of Colonel David Shepherd, on December 8, 1795.[15] Jacob and Ruhama Shepherd Wetzel's children were: Sabra, born February 22, 1798, and died January 20, 1822. Sabra married Dr. Charles Newton and they had one daughter, Amanda, who died in 1821 at the age of two years.[16] Cyrus Wetzel, son of Jacob and Ruhama Wetzel, born December 1, 1800, married Elizabeth Mills. They had two sons, Jacob and Francis; both died unmarried, and one daughter, Sarah

10. Martin Wetzel, his wife, Mary Wetzel, and his daughters, Barbary, Catherine, Rhuie and Alexander Caldwell's family, are all buried in the McCreary cemetery three miles east of U. S. 250 in Marshall County, West Virginia.
11. John T. McCreary's grandfather was the undertaker that buried Martin Wetzel in October 1829.
12. Lewis Wetzel's mother, Mary Bonnett Wetzel, died in June, 1805, on Wheeling Creek in the old home place, owned by her son Jacob Wetzel adjoining Ezekiel Caldwell's and was buried in the McCreary cemetery, as was John Wetzel, Jr., and his family. Mary Bonnett Wetzel was born in 1735. Bonnett to Draper, *Draper's Mss.*, 24S47 and 2E23 in the State Historical Society of Wisconsin, Madison, Wisconsin.
13. Bonnett to Draper, *Draper's Mss. 24S49*, in State Historical Society of Wisconsin, Madison, Wisconsin. Jacob Wolf was from Preston County, West Virginia.
14. Perhaps others but names are unknown.
15. Bonnett to Draper, *Draper's Mss. 20S103*, in State Historical Society of Wisconsin, Madison, Wisconsin.
16. *Ibid.*, 20S104.

Melvina, who married W. N. McKinsey, (also called Mackenzie.) Emily Wetzel, daughter of Jacob and Ruhama Wetzel, married W. H. H. Pinney; they had no children. Maria Wetzel, daughter of Jacob and Ruhama Wetzel, married David Allen and had the following children: Elma, Corrina, Thirza, and Austin.

Eliza Wetzel, daughter of Jacob and Ruhama Wetzel, married James S. Kelly and had the following children: Amanda, Nancy, Oscar, and William. Amanda married Ezra Allman.

J. Hiram Wetzel, son of Jacob and Ruhama Wetzel, married Alzada Aldrich and had one son, Jacob.[17]

Susan Wetzel, daughter of Jacob and Ruhama Wetzel, married Thomas Lou and had two daughters, Caroline and Adaline.

Sarah Wetzel, daughter of Jacob and Ruhama Wetzel, married Isaac Briggs and had two children, Mary and David. Mary married Thomas Stewart. Sarah was born May 20, 1810, and died October 17, 1880, and is buried in the cemetery at Carrollton, Ohio.

Susannah Wetzel, daughter of John and Mary Bonnett Wetzel, married Nathan Goodrich, (often called Guttery.) Their children were: John, near Brookfield, Indiana; James, near St. Louis, Missouri; Cynthia married John Cherry near Shelbysville, Indiana; Susan, marriage unknown; George, the eldest son, married Mary Tush.[18]

John Wetzel, Jr., son of John and Mary Bonnett Wetzel, married Eleanor Williams, daughter of Thomas, sister of Hugh, George and Jonathan Williams of Bedford County, Pennsylvania. They had two sons and seven daughters: George, Lewis, Polly, Ruth, Keziah, Sophia, Eleanor, Eliza, and Barbara. George, who was born in 1797, was living

---

17. There may have been others but they are unknown.
18. Bonnett to Draper, *Draper's Mss. 24S49*, in State Historical Society of Wisconsin, Madison, Wisconsin.

in Appanoose County, Iowa, when interviewed in 1868 by Lyman C. Draper.[19]

Polly married Nathaniel Kane; Ruth married Adam Coffield on October 24, 1828, with Thomas Dakan performing the ceremony. Keziah unmarried; Eliza married William Rohrbrough; Sophia married, name not given, died soon after marriage. Eleanor married James McCreary; Barbara died unmarried; Lewis had no children and lived near Dayton, Ohio.[20]

The Bonnett Family

Catharine, Mary, Lewis,[21] Susannah, John, and Samuel Bonnett were brothers and sisters, and children of John Bonnett, Sr.

Catharine Bonnett married John C. Sickes (or Sycks) and had the following children: Philip, David, and Margaret.

Mary Bonnett married Captain John Wetzel. Their children are previously named in this chapter.

Lewis Bonnett married Elizabeth Waggoner and had the following children: Lewis, Jr., born in 1778, John, Mary, Elizabeth, and Barbara. Lewis Bonnett, Jr., married Jane McClain.[21]

Jane Bonnett, daughter of Lewis Bonnett, Jr., and Jane McClain Bonnett, married Frederick Williams, and had the following children: Mary Ellen and Margaret Belle. Mary Ellen Williams married Louis Wagner; they had one son, Frank Wagner. Margaret Belle Williams married Frank W. Bowers,[21] and their children are: George W. Bowers, Ella Mae Bowers, and Charles Albert Bowers.

Susannah Bonnett never married.

John[21] and Samuel Bonnett's marriages are unknown;

---

19. *Ibid.*, 24S41.
20. *Ibid.*, 24S52.
21. John Bonnett, Jr., was born in August, 1735, and died Sept. 2, 1816, aged 81 years and one month. Lewis Bonnett, Sr., was born in 1737 and died March 9, 1808, aged 71 years. Jane McClain Bonnett was born in 1780 and died August 20, 1839, aged 59 years. Jane Bonnett Williams died in 1925 and her husband, Frederick Williams, died in 1907. (See Appendices.) Frank W. Bowers died in October, 1938.

but John Bonnett, Jr., had the following children: Lewis, Eve, Benjamin, Elizabeth, and Simon. Lewis Bonnett, son of John Bonnett, who was the son of Lewis Bonnett, the second, married Fannie Miller in 1824.[22] Daniel Blue married Eve Bonnett, daughter of John Bonnett in 1817.[23]

Lewis Bonnett, Sr., was born in Paoli, Chester County, Pennsylvania, in 1737. His ancestors emigrated from French Flanders and were of French extraction. They set-

Bonnett Home on Big Wheeling Creek

tled at Paoli, Pennsylvania, where his parents both died within a few years of each other. Lewis Bonnett, Sr., had one brother, Samuel Bonnett, who took charge of the family after the parents' death, and moved them to the Monongahela country. In the fall of that same year he was killed by the fall of a tree. Lewis Bonnett, Sr., enlisted into what

22. *Marriage License Book 1, p. 50,* found in the Clerk of the County Court's Office at Wheeling, West Virginia.
23. *Marriage License Book 1, p. 32,* found in the Clerk of the County Court's Office in the Courthouse at Wheeling, West Virginia; also see Appendices.

was then called the Virginia Rangers, and was under Washington in Braddock's defeat. He was then about 18 years of age. He was not in Bouquet's expedition of 1764.

He married Elizabeth Waggoner in the South Branch and took a part in all the Indian scouting parties. He moved to Wheeling Creek with his brother-in-law John Wetzel in 1764, where he lived for a few years. He sold his property on Wheeling Creek and moved to the mouth of Dunkard Creek on the Monongahela where he lived for several years. Selling out there he moved back to Wheeling Creek, Virginia, about 1781 or perhaps 1782, and died at his residence there March 9, 1808. He is buried on the farm in a family cemetery.

Elizabeth Waggoner Bonnett's ancestors migrated from Flanders about the same time as Lewis Bonnett's and settled on the South Branch. Her father built a small fort, and one day the old man, his son Peter, and his daughter, Mary, were working in the field when the Indians came upon them, killing the old man and taking the boy and girl captives. The Indians rightly judged that they would be followed by the Whites, divided their party; each taking a prisoner. When the Whites pursued they happened to take the trail of the party that had Mary, who was a young woman, and two or three horses. It was early the next morning that the Whites overtook them. They fired at the Indians while they were still around their campfire, killing one Indian, wounding another, but unluckily one of the bullets proved fatal to "poor Mary". She was accidentally shot through the body and died the next day.

Mary was to have been married in a few days to a young man named Peters. He lamented "poor Mary's fate". However, he remained with the family for some time and finally went to Montreal, Canada, with some Frenchmen, where he remained for awhile. He then made his way to Philadelphia, and bound himself out to boot and shoe making. He married and lived there until his death.

Elizabeth Waggoner Bonnett had a younger brother, John Waggoner, who moved to the Monongahela, married, and had his family destroyed by the Indians. She had a young sister, Barbara, who died at the ripe old age of 80, in the Monongahela country.

Lewis Bonnett, Sr., had three sisters. John C. Sykes (or Sickes) married the eldest sister, Catharine. Captain John Wetzel married the second sister, Mary. The third one, Susannah, never married, but lived an old maid and

Stone Barn on the Bonnett Farm

died in Shenandoah County, Virginia. Old John C. Sykes (or Sickes) never lived on Wheeling Creek, Virginia. He remained in the Monongahela country and died there.

Sickes had three sons, Henry, Phillip, and David, who went West and settled near Natchez, Miss. Philip remained there, but David went to Texas and settled there on the Brazos river. Henry married Barbary Selsor and lived and died in Monongahela Township, Greene Co., Penn.

John C. Sickes had a daughter named Margaret, cap-tured by the Indians, and taken as a prisoner to their towns.

After some years she was taken to Detroit, where she married a white man who later took part with the Indians against General Wayne, and was killed in that battle. Margaret then made application once more to get back to her native country, which was granted her. She and her four children came back safely to her friends after an absence of many years. It is true that she always had a friendly feeling for the Indians and she would try to defend them when the Whites would say all manner of evil about them.[24]

The tales of Wetzel's daring, hereinafter described, are those gathered from original and authentic records, and those handed down from generation to generation in the family,[25] and pieced out in places where both tradition and history are silent, from the author's imagination. The latter is the case in describing the trip from eastern Pennsylvania to the Ohio river.

Cecil B. Hartley, in his *Life of Lewis Wetzel,* says: "The carelessness of those who knew these men and the disturbed state of the country has occasioned the loss of nearly all written record of their action."

In the main the story is true as far as we can determine. It is written neither to praise nor to blame the central figure, but to picture him as he was and in so doing to shed some light on border days.[26]

---

24. Bonnett to Draper, *Draper's Mss., 11E34 and 11E35,* of the State Historical Society of Wisconsin, Madison, Wisconsin. Henry was born Feb. 12, 1757, and served in the Revolutionary War.

25. In preparing this story, in addition to family traditions and written records, the following were consulted: Eli Huggins, 92-year-old descendant of the Wetzels; John T. Wetzel, the grandson of Martin Wetzel and a great grandson of Captain John Wetzel; W. Scott Powell, author of the *History of Marshall County,* T. S. Terrill, aged 98; S. R. Hanen, aged 99; J. H. Hill, aged 96. (See Bibliography.)

26. Where authorities differ, as they sometimes do, I have chosen the most authentic and probable version to give readers.

CHAPTER II

NO CONCRETE highways spanned the state, no trolleys; the wooded hills of Pennsylvania had never echoed the shrill blast of an approaching train, not even a Conestoga wagon had ever creaked up the rocky roads over the Tuscarora Mountain, for there was no modern road, when honest John Wetzel of Lancaster County in the year 1764 gathered his family and with a few other families prepared to cross the Alleghenies in search of opportunity and a home.

The neighbors came to say good-bye and to advise the travelers not to go. Old men with pipes in their mouths, women with pleasant faces, bright and happy children, young men and women—all came to wish the Wetzels good luck, but doubted if they would have it. The long, tedious trip was portrayed, the dangers from Indians dwelt upon and the uncertainty of finding anything in the end stressed. But John Wetzel was a stubborn Dutchman. Having set his hand to the plow he had no intention of turning back.

Two oxen were hitched to a wagon, the belongings of the family piled on, a seven-year-old boy (Martin) on the seat beside his father, Mrs. Wetzel, Christiana, Lewis, and George were made as comfortable as possible in the wagon bed.

"Are you not afraid of Indians?" asked a neighbor.

"The Indians," said honest John, "are not God Almighty. They are only men like myself—less than myself, because of their ignorance, perfidy and untruth. We place them on a plane with Deity in fearing them. We should not fear the devil and his works."

Turning to the baby Lewis he remarked, "If we remain here this child will always be as poor as I am."

Mrs. Wetzel apparently was a model wife, for she answered the neighbors' advice by saying to her husband, "Whither thou goest I will go; and where thou lodgest I will lodge." She pressed the baby to her cheek to hide the tears at parting from life-long friends. The women kissed her and the children, crying over little Lewis. "Oh, the Injuns'll eat him," said one. "Or he will eat the Injuns," said honest John, now anxious to be off.

"Ahem! ahem!" The resonant voice of the old red-faced justice of the peace arrested attention.

"Ahem! Listen to me."

"Yes. Listen to the wise old justice," shouted the crowd.

"John Wetzel," said the justice. "I am wise. Are you? You may go away from all you know, out to the wild lands that you do not know. You leave a house for no house. Your wife, your son, your baby — what will become of them? Can they make buzzard savory? Can they drink Indian? Nay, John, you cannot go. I am wise. I cannot help being so."

"I never set up for a wiseacre," said John, picking up the ox whip.

A woman named Lizzie Pheister wrapped a flag of Great Britain around little Lewis to keep him warm.

"You've made an Indian of him already with all this bright red," said John. "Get up!" The oxen cocked their ears toward the west, the wagon creaked, others fell in behind, and the little caravan started down a slightly rutted road that soon lost itself in the woods.

The team trudged on. The shallow ruts in the road grew fainter until they disappeared and a leaf-strewn trail wound among the ancient trees, making soft footing for the faithful beasts and fairly easy riding for the occupants of the wagon except when the wheels struck a projecting root and jolted the contents. Mother Wetzel watched the slow procession of majestic tree trunks passing in review, uncounted markers measuring the distance from home and friends and girlhood memories.

The primeval forest is friendly to those attuned to its moods or conscious of its unspoiled beauty. But the endless expanse of trees and the unbroken solitude, the constant irritation of the rough road, the whipping of branches across one's face and the lonesome murmur of rustling leaves may be anything but cheerful to one accustomed to the security and comfort of civilized ways.

A tear fell on the British flag as the young mother valiantly strove to control her feelings. Wiping her misty eyes the faithful wife tried hard to fulfill cheerfully her promise of "whither thou goest—" The broad back of John carefully guiding the team offered no sympathy. Always trees and trees, and who knew the end? It was too much. The mother of Lewis Wetzel, Indian killer and strong man of the frontier, gathered her infant to her face and wept until the folds of England's flag were soaked with tears.

Ashamed of her weakness, but feeling better for it, the woman, whose Teutonic ancestors had gone forth with their men to conquer mighty Rome, brushed aside the signs of grief and said, "My tears have wetted all this pretty flag Aunt Lizzie Pheister gave Lewis."

John, who was busy steering the team around the roughest roots, and who was not much given to sentiment anyway, replied, "That flag has caused more trouble and tears than it is worth. We will have it no longer." He tore it from his baby and threw it at the feet of his oxen. The rumblings of the Revolutionary War had not reached the backwoods of Pennsylvania, but John Wetzel had shown his personal ideas about loyalty to King George, and perhaps to all restraint. His bridges were burned behind him, and he felt confident of dealing with the future when it arrived.

The party included the Wetzels, the Bonnetts, the Zanes, the Eberly and the Rosencranz families. They were headed for free land of reputed promise in the Wheeling Creek wilderness. Eberly and Rosencranz, having made the trip before, had returned to bring their families. They pictured a land of opportunity and had little trouble in persuading John Wetzel that his present holdings of two hogs, a cow and a garden space offered little inducement for a man of ambition, when a fertile empire, untouched by the plow, awaited claimers in the West. The Zanes, founders of Wheeling, joined the train of emigrants for exploring purposes.

Cogitating on these things and recalling with relief the small sacrifice he was making and the fortune he expected to make John let the oxen ramble down a little slope as the wagon urged them on. Like a rocket from the ground and with the roar of an airplane a ruffed grouse split a tangle of rhododendron by the wayside, darted around the scraggy top of a struggling pine and disappeared among the distant oak tops.

With a bound like jack-rabbits the team was off, scampering down the grade with wagon rumbling, pans and kettles rattling and young Martin's eyes nearly popping from his head. A guttural command and the heavy hand of John on the biting whip which flicked their faces eased the team to a walk and then a stop until the rest of the train caught up. Somewhat breathless from excitement and relieved at the slightness of the danger the travelers proceeded in better spirits. For the episode broke the restraint that had clung to the party since its start.

Baby Lewis slept in spite of the jouncing of his bed. Martin begged to drive, and his father granted the privilege, watching with pride and amusement the serious attention the child gave to the business, little dreaming that those grave eyes and clenched hands would some day sight and hurl the tomahawk with a skill surpassing that of the redman and an aim so true as to make the name of Martin Wetzel spoken with awe around frontier hearthstones.

Camp was made near a convenient spring. After the meal the party gathered around a small bonfire of brush

and branches from a dead tree, talking over the events of
the day and wondering about road conditions for the morrow.   Mrs. Wetzel spread a blanket and laid little Lewis
on it.   With the firelight playing over his pudgy form he
kicked his feet and waved his arms in animal joy at the
warmth and light.   Mrs. Eberly hummed a tune to be
joined by others until the glade resounded with the plain-

"Baby Lewis caught the redman's eye as the arrow was fitted to the
string and the bow drawn back."

tive strains of an old folk song.   Far up the valley rolled
the sound as the lusty Dutchmen put heart and soul into
music that they could not express in prose.

Crouched in the shelter of a projecting rock a Shawnee
munched dried corn from his bare hand.   The notes of har-
mony—unusual sound—reached his keen ears.   With the
stealth of a fox he was up and moving in the direction of

the music. Soon a pair of beady eyes peeking from a clump of elder, unseen by all the noisy campers, was viewing the scene in all its details.

Softly an arrow was fitted to the string, the bow drawn back—and Lewis Wetzel, kicking in childish glee, caught the redman's eye. His mind shot back to a wigwam on the Kanawha. A papoose on its back was fighting imaginary foes with hands and feet. The bow cord loosened, and with a grunt of disdain at his own weakness the redman faded into the night from which he came.

Topping the summit of a long hard hill one day the train stopped to view the sea of green-clad hills and valleys spread out before them. A thin smoke column arising from what appeared to be a clearing attracted their attention. Hurrying down the trail they approached the spot with anticipation of a bare but sincere welcome and the pleasure of seeing people again. Around a dense wall of evergreens they came suddenly into the clearing, but not to see the fresh-hewn logs of a cabin or the form of owners moving about. The smoke arose from sizzling embers where a cabin had stood.

Slowly the truth dawned on the gazing home-seekers. "Injuns!" whispered Mrs. Rosencranz. Mother Wetzel clutched her baby closer, while the color left her cheeks. Here a man had sought a home and found the end to worldly ambitions at the hand of roving savages. Looking around one of the Zane boys found gruesome proof of the tragedy. Still in death the pioneer grasped the axe with which he had been sharpening fence posts when a tomahawk cleft his skull. No sign of other inhabitants was visible, but a piece of cloth caught on a stub where the clearing met the woods indicated that a woman had been taken away by the Indians. Farther in the forest a low spot of ground showed the imprint of several moccasined feet.

The emigrant train moved on with its best speed anxious to leave the spot if not the memory of the smoking cabin in the clearing. The oxen trudged on, the wagons creaked and the red squirrels from precarious perches at safe distances scolded the intruders of their domain. The travelers saw them not; their minds were back with the man and his axe, their eyes and ears alert to movement behind the screen of undergrowth that lined the way. They spoke in lowered voices, heard sounds that did not exist and saw in distant glimpse of white birch trunk the sunlight glinting on musket barrel or eagle plume.

At noon the party stopped for lunch without a fire. John Wetzel was just leading his team back from a creek where he had taken them to water, when without warning an old wrinkled man walked from the woods. Two guns were pointed at his breast while one of the Whites grasped the handle of a hoe that protruded from his wagon. The old man raised his hand in sign of peace. "No shoot. Friend," said he. It was plain from dress and copper skin that he was an Indian, although far advanced in years beyond the warrior age.

"No danger. Alone," he assured the nervous Whites, complacently seating himself on a half-rotten log near one of the wagons.

"Why go——" waving a withered hand in the general direction the travelers were headed. "White man's land ——," pointing to the East.

"We go to make homes on free land in the West," explained one of the Whites.

"Indian's land," said the savage.

"Our government has bought it from your chiefs," he was told.

"Can chiefs sell air? Can government buy song of birds or speed of deer? White man sell rum; make warriors crazy. Chop down trees; drive game away. Kill Indians; lie to chiefs. Beware! The leaves fall in winter, but come again in spring. When the tom-tom beats for the war dance red warriors come as leaves in spring. White man go back. Save lives."

But the Whites were not impressed by the feeble arguments of the old man. They recalled the smoking cabin and resolved if occasion should arise, that they be not slow to avenge. Was not this land theirs by treaty or purchase? And were not all Indians to be despised for their "ignorance, perfidy and untruth"? As the old man shuffled off with a shake of his head John hitched up his team and gave the order to move on.

The settlement at what is now Wheeling, W. Va., was reached at last, much to the relief of everybody, especially the women, who had much to tell about the discomforts of their trip and much to be told by women of the settlement about frontier life and the people who were making it. And here the writer is supported by written or spoken records of what took place. Bonnetts, Eberly and Rosencranz had picked out a place on Wheeling Creek where they planned to make their new homes. They expected the Wetzels to settle there with them."

"No," said John, in reply to the invitation. "There are too many here now." Having come this far he proposed to keep going until he found a spot to his liking that included plenty of room. Land lay all around them. Why be cramped as in the East?

"But the danger of Indians," he was reminded.

"Had I been afraid of Indians I should never come here," was Wetzel's answer.

"You know little about Indians," said Eberly.

"I know a good deal about white men," replied John. If more white men had held this view of things many scalps which adorned tepee poles might have stuck with their original owners to their graves. But the Whites in general considered the Indians an inferior people, unnecessary to try to understand and not possessing rights to be regarded so carefully as their own desires.

"Wetzel, you are strange and do not see the wisdom of settling with us here," said Bonnett.

"I do not see the wisdom; it may be yours; it is not mine. Good-bye."

"Good-bye."

Giving the oxen a slap with the whip the hardy man drove on until he came to a spot that pleased him. It was on Big Wheeling Creek (Sand Hill District), Marshall County, W. Va., fourteen miles from the Ohio River.

"You are not afraid?" he said to his wife as she got out of the wagon and looked around.

The first home the Wetzel's built in Marshall County

"What is there to be afraid of?" she replied, holding little Lewis closer to her. Had the memory of the smoking cabin vanished from her mind, or had the dutiful wife who promised to go "whither thou goest" hid her fear to make a home for her family? She put the baby in the wagon and with Martin "helping" set about making a fire and preparing a meal.

"Thank God," said John Wetzel reverently. "We are free!" Free from the restraints of civilization, the craft of greedy men, the gossip of petty neighbors. Free as the wild animals of the woods or the fish in the streams, also as exposed to danger as them and as oblivious of the fact. For freedom has its price, as does everything else; and the price of freedom is fear. Fear so constant as to be forgotten, perhaps, but present nevertheless. A fawn is as free as a flight of fancy, but it lives in fear of the wolf or the panther. So the pioneers who lived in the border land between the established settlements of the Whites and the remote territory of the Reds had the joy of their freedom tempered by the fear of a visit by painted warriors.

No high-strung, nervous, hysterical fear was this. Leave that for the effete beaus of eastern towns or sheltered women in old communities, but an unconscious fear taken as a matter of course like wet feet and cold mush for lunch. Happily the pioneer did not know that he lived in a state of fear, but it was hard on the redman who found the white brother quick on the trigger, slow to understand the Indian's viewpoint but ready to take "an eye for an eye" if some irresponsible rumcrazed Indian stole his horse or murdered his wife.

John Wetzel doubtless never thought of fear, for he built his cabin where it was exposed on all sides to incursions from the Indians and was beyond reach of the fort at Wheeling in case of attack.

CHAPTER III

TIME went on and the little pioneer family felt more and more secure. Visitors were rare. Sometimes a white hunter sauntered by, stopping to talk of crops or game supply. An occasional Indian or squaw dropped in to trade dry venison for tobacco or powder.

John was content and showed no longing for other people than his family. He rarely went to the settlement for supplies, and his wife never went. She was busy, as her family grew in number as well as size. Three additional children came to take the mother's mind from Indian tales or old-time memories. When Jacob, Susannah, and John, Jr., arrived in succession, with Martin, Christiana, George and Lewis the offspring numbered seven, making a snug little settlement of their own.

Lewis Wetzel took to frontier life like a duck to water. He thrilled to tales of Indian raids and white reprisals, as they drifted in to the remote cabin from chance callers or were heard by his father during trips to the settlement. When the boy was about ten years old a man, named Daniel Greathouse, leading a gang of ruffians, killed some friendly Indians—a popular sport at the time. Other Indians went on the warpath about it, and young Lewis listened to accounts of the affairs with keenest interest.

His work with his father toughened the youngster's frame, taught him the ways of the woods and welded an affection for the man that may explain the famous Wetzel oath of revenge later, and its fulfillment through many bloody years.

John, the elder, had an eye for business and rounded up a lot of "wild horses". From his viewpoint they were worthless and he was reclaiming them. The Indians thought differently and stole some of the horses, causing him much annoyance. One day a redskin came to Wetzel's place and got into an argument with John about the horses, now numbering around 100 head. Apparently his argument did not impress the Dutchman much, for the Indian threatened vengeance. Young Lewis then jumped into the picture, throwing a stone at the Indian for the indignity offered the father.

When the Reds claimed that the Whites stole their land, John countered with the information that the Indians were letting it go to waste anyway, thus inferring that their alleged ownership was not to be taken seriously.

Dressed in deerskin and woolen clothes of his mother's making, sitting before blazing logs in the open fireplace, young Lewis thought over these things, while growing muscles cried for action. Adventure called and the old spirit which moved honest John to leave Lancaster County urged his son to action, wherever it might be.

War broke out—the Revolutionary War. Lewis, but a child in years—he was 13 in 1776—begged to go and help the rebels lick the King. Deprived of this privilege he and Jacob staged mimic warfare at their play, educating themselves in the slyness of the savage and the courage of the White. As the War advanced the Indians became more hostile. Frequent attacks on the Whites were reported. In the midst of these unhealthy rumors and forays the dread disease, smallpox, fastened itself on Lewis, and the rest of the family caught it from him.

With no vaccination, no hospitals, no nurses and no learned doctors the sick folks of the backwoods those days had to live or die unaided. The Wetzel children lived.

Indians were up in arms. The Revolutionary War was in full swing. While England attacked the colonists' army in the East, Indians kept the frontier folks on edge in the

West. Painted war parties were coming nearer and nearer the Wheeling settlements. Mrs. Wetzel begged John to move to a settlement, but he still knew no fear.

"If anything happens to me Martin is almost a man and can take my responsibility," said the stubborn emigrant. Little did he realize that Martin was to have the job.

One day in August of 1776 John Wetzel went to the settlement for some powder and to get the news. He was keeping posted on conditions, even if he did not let his family know his fears. Formerly he had told his wife everything. Now-a-days he was silent when he came home. This time after the father left, Martin wandered off with his gun to look for a bear he had seen a few days before in the woods near the cornfield. Lewis stayed home with his mother and the children. Time dragged. All were rather anxious. Long before John returned Lewis was out on a knoll watching for his father. At sundown the man appeared. To Lewis' question about news at the fort his father replied, "Not so good to-day."

When they got to the cabin Martin had returned.

"Where is the bear?" asked Lewis.

"He dodged me when he saw me," said Martin.

"That is a queer bear," remarked John.

"I don't think it is a bear, but an Indian," said Lewis.

"It is a bear skin," replied Martin.

"Then it must be a bear," thought John.

"I think it's an Indian in a bear's skin," ventured Lewis.

"Lewis! Such nonsense," cried the mother.

When the doors were closed for the night and the mother was reading the Bible to the family a queer noise was heard outside. "What is that?" asked Mrs. Wetzel, with her finger on the word where she had stopped.

"Go on," the husband replied. "It was only a rustling of the wind."

She took up her reading again for about fifteen minutes, when an exclamation from Lewis attracted her. She looked

up. Her husband was at the door, his eye at a knothole.
"Why John Wetzel," she began.

"Hush!!" he whispered. There was a rustling outside.

"It's the old bear," she said.

"Come here," hissed John.

She went to him, placed her eye to the knothole and
saw a shadow moving outside. "What is it?" she whispered.

"An Indian," was his guarded reply. "Hand me the
gun."

John eased the barrel through the hole and fired. A
shriek from outside echoed the report that filled the room.

"What have you done?" wailed the wife, wringing her
hands.

John had killed the bear that had been seen around the
cornfield and that Martin had hunted all day. It proved
to be an Indian in a bear's skin, showing that Lewis' suspicions were correct. No investigation is reported of this
event. Neither coroner nor game warden asked embarrassing questions. Indians were neither game nor human
apparently.[27]

Lewis and Jacob Wetzel's Captivity in 1776.[28]

I will relate it as my two cousins, Lewis and Jacob
Wetzel told me themselves.

The settlers at Wheeling Creek had retired to Shepherd's Fort that season and the two boys were sent home
to their farm to plow and hoe some corn. Lewis being the
older took his father's rifle and powder horn along.

One plowed and the other hoed corn all day. They took
up their abode in the house for the night. In the morning
Jacob began to prepare preakfast. Lewis went out to get
the horse which was turned in a pasture lot the evening

27. From R. C. V. Myer's, "Wetzel the Scout."
28. Lewis Bonnett to Lyman C. Draper, June 30, 1847. Draper's
Mss. 11E96, 11E97, 11E98, 11E99, of the State Historical Society of
Wisconsin, Madison, Wisconsin.

before, with a bell on. Lewis, having the bridle hung on his arm, stepped out into the yard and was walking straight in the direction of the pasture. The Indians in the meantime lay concealed behind the fence right in front of the house so that they might the better shoot right into the door, when it was opened. They took deliberate aim at Lewis' breast, and in the act of pulling the trigger of their guns the horse luckily happened to shake his head in a contrary direction. Lewis instantly wheeled or turned in the direction of the bell. The Indian in the same instant pulled the trigger. One ball passed along his breast bone, fracturing a piece of the breast bone, but did not enter under the bone. Another ball passed through his shirt sleeve close by his shoulder, but it did no harm. Lewis ran to get into the house but one or two Indians were concealed behind the corner of the meat and milkhouse. They instantly sprang to the door and prevented Lewis from entering. They soon made a prisoner of, "poor little Jacob." Lewis ran with all his might through the cornfield, but to his misfortune on the lower side of the cornfield was a steep bank. His foot slipped and he fell prostrate. Before he could recover himself the Indians had hold of him. His wound bled profusely so that the blood was seen sticking on the corn blades the next day. The Indian that caught him led him back to the house and claimed Lewis as his prisoner. The Indian took sassafras leaves, chewed and pounded them and bound them on his wound, which soon stopped the bleeding for awhile.

The Indian that captured Lewis also claimed his father's rifle gun, after he had ascertained that it belonged to the senior Wetzel. They soon bound the boys' hands behind their backs and all things were ready for moving. Jacob while in the act of being tied begged liberty to take the pot off the fire with meat in it for their breakfast, which was granted the boy. He set the pot down beside the dresser. The Indian then fastened the cord around his wrists, and when he had finished tying the boy the same Indian took the pot, carried it out of doors and dashed it down on the step stone before the door, breaking it into a thousand pieces.

The Indians then took their captive boys and made their way to the Ohio River some miles below Wheeling where their canoes were hid in the willow bushes. All safely over they started for the Big Lick on McMahon's Creek about 20 miles from the Ohio River, and for their wigwams on the Muskingum.

Thirteen-year-old Lewis Wetzel, child of the frontier, tough as a waterbeach and stubborn as one of the oxen which hauled him across the Alleghenies, was a captive of the dreaded and despised Indians. His childish mind fired with hatred for the redmen and his vivid imagination nourished on tales of atrocities, he was torn between dread of the scowling warriors who switched his legs to make him hurry and elation at the distinction of adventure with the cruel natives. Blood streamed from his wound as he trudged stoically on.

"White boy bleeds easy," observed a chief. "His blood is thin." He grasped the lad by the hair and gave him a thrust forward. No sound escaped the tightened lips. "Good," cried the chief. "White boy no coward. He will be chief yet. If he will not be chief he will roast."

When their arms were bound with thongs little eleven-year-old Jacob wept with pain but Lewis never winced. It was the code of the borderland, and Lewis would not be found wanting when his hour of trial was at hand.

Tradition says that the boys' legs were bound at the knees, and the youngsters forced into a jog trot, but this writer is of the opinion that some of the old story tellers used their imaginations at this point. How could a couple of boys with their legs tied at the knees keep up with a band of Indians hurrying to get out of the country with their captives?

"They're taking us from home," wailed little Jacob, clinging to his brother. A blow from a brave separated the boys. For two days the Indians drove their captives like stolen sheep, tormenting them continually. Jacob cried much of the time, but Lewis paid no attention, his hatred for the reds feeding on the treatment.

The first night the Indians being much fatigued fastened a cord around each of the boys' waists, and made the boys lie down. The Indians then fastened the cord to the saplings. The second night out the Indians camped on McMahon's Creek in what is now the state of Ohio. "White boy hungry?" they asked, holding up tempting morsels of deer flesh before the famished children's eyes. The Indians made a bright fire and smoked until what to the anxious boys seemed a late hour. One by one they slumped down in slumber. Lewis watched them like a hawk. He and Jacob were tied together. Presently one of the guards noticed Lewis' eyes shining in the dark. He came up frowning and said, "White boy sleep". Lewis made no reply.

"White boy sleep," repeated the guard, kicking him in the face as a reminder. "Now sleep, or Indian cut eyes out to make him sleep." At this broad hint Lewis closed his eyes and apparently slept beside his brother.

The next night the Indians gorged themselves with the single meal of the day. As the camp fire burned low one by one the redmen rolled over heavily and slept. Lewis began to rub down the cords over his hips. One of the Indians awoke and asked him what he wanted, Lewis told him a drink, and the Indian arose and gave the boy a drink from a little brass kettle that they had taken from the Wetzel home. Before the Indian lay down the second time he fastened the cords tighter around the boys. Lewis swelled himself out saying, too tight, and Jacob catching the hint, did the same thing. The Indian then slackened the cord and that made it much looser than before.

The Indian lay down again and was soon fast asleep. He was no sooner snoring than Lewis began to rub the cords down over his hips and soon loosened himself.

He whispered to Jacob to do the same thing and get up. "We will go home." Trembling the little fellow obeyed. With the stealth of cats they threaded their way between the sleeping braves, aided by the dim glow of the hot ashes. As the leaves crumpled under their feet they paused, but no one awoke. Finding a hulky brave directly in their path, Lewis pretended to fix the fire until he made sure that all were sound asleep.

"Over," whispered Lewis as he lifted his brother across the body and stepped gingerly after him. They had crossed the outer circle of Indians and the dense forest lay before them.

No panic-stricken dash for freedom followed. Lewis Wetzel, although but a boy, was as cool as if stalking a deer. They went a hundred yards and sat down on a log. The cold damp earth against their bare feet reminded them that they had no shoes on.

"We cannot go on," said Jacob.

"Not barefooted," said Lewis. "We must have some moccasins".

"You stay here and I will get them," spoke the elder in a tone that must be obeyed. He stole again to the campfire, crossing the sleeping Indians, body after body. Two pairs of moccasins by the fire to dry caught his eye. Snatching them up he made his way back to Jacob shivering on the log. They put the moccasins on when Lewis said, "Now don't move. Stay here until I come back".

"Where are you going?" whimpered Jacob.

"We must have a gun", replied the older boy, still cool as a cucumber and enjoying his feeling of ability to cope with the situation and stimulated by success thus far. So back to the enemies' camp the second time went Lewis, picking his steps with the care and skill he had learned through stalking game and with nerves as tight as harp strings.

His father's gun was leaning against a tree beside a sleeping brave. Lewis picked it up. The Indian stirred.

The white boy held his breath. It was a fateful moment, but the redskin heard no sound and slept again. In a jiffy Lewis was back to his brother on the log.

A fourth time Lewis went back and secured his father's powder horn hanging on a little limb of the tree against which the gun was leaning.

Without a word the two struck out, making all speed possible with discretion. The Indian sleeping beside the gun Lewis had taken must have awakened and discovered his loss, for in a couple of hours the keen ears of Lewis de-

Lewis and Jacob Wetzel's escape from the Indians.

tected the sounds of pursuers on their trail. Closer and closer they came. Frantic flight would only draw them on. "Down", whispered Lewis. The boys hid in the sea of tall grass around them. Like "frozen" rabbits they lay, while the Indians came on and passed. "Up", said the elder boy. He and his brother fell in behind the Indians and followed the pursuers toward liberty.

Soon the redskins stopped. So did the boys. As the disgusted braves came back toward them the fugitives could hear them cursing the guards and everybody for the loss of two captives who had stolen a gun, powder horn, and two pair of moccasins, and were only boys at that.

A hollow tree was handy and the two boys pushed into its dark shelter. For the second time the Indians passed them by. As the sound of baffled pursuers died away the white boys came from their hiding place and made tracks for the Ohio river.

However, the redmen were not to be eluded so easily. The next day two of them were detailed to follow on horses and recapture the boys. Again they underestimated the woodcraft and pluck of the youngsters. Hiding in a clump of bushes the lads watched the mounted warriors lose their trail and give up the chase. The gun which Lewis risked his life to get back from the Indians did not prove of much service to the travelers, for the farsighted boy refused to use it on game, since he had powder but no bullet for a second load, and wanted to be prepared for an emergency in case Indians confronted them. The boys lived for days on roots while making their way back to civilization. They finally reached the Ohio river a little below Wheeling Island and began to plan ways to cross. Each one got some dry logs and fastened them together with bark. They took off their clothes, fastened them on top of the logs; they trusted their feet for paddles, as they steered the logs with their hands, descending a little down stream. They set off together, Jacob kicking with all his might. Lewis told him to kick slower. In spite of this, Jacob landed about a hun-

dred yards above Lewis. They put on their dry clothing
and Lewis shouldered his father's rifle gun, and with pomp
and joy marched up the river bank at the mouth of Wheeling Creek and soon arrived at Fort Henry at Wheeling.
When they walked into the settlement at Wheeling a crowd
gathered to hear of their capture and escape. All listened
with profound silence to their story. Lewis said if he could
have got the gun he would have fought to the last rather
than be taken by "Infernal Indians". Bertha Rosencranz
seeing the dried blood on him and getting some lint for his
wounds, said, "Lewis is hurt in the breast".

"Never mind the hurt", said Lewis, true to type and
looking very fierce.

It is a little hard for us to-day to understand the popular attitude of the frontiersmen toward the Indian. Fearful of his treachery and respectful of his cunning, they
lived in a state of apprehension, submerging their dread
with a front of boldness and feeding their hatred on an
ambition that must realize the fortunes of the white race
meant the funerals of the red. With no governmental restraint on the one hand and a living menace on the other
the instinct of self-preservation brought personal and public opinion to regard the native as a thing to be hated as
only fear can hate.

The boy Lewis, imbued with the philosophy of the border and having tasted the torture of the heartless redskin,
on reaching the shelter of his home, threw the Indian's
musket from his shoulder and raising his clenched fist cried,
"I swear to kill every Indian that crosses my path so long
as God lets me live." Anger and defiance stilled the pain
of his wound as every fiber of the slender frame trembled
with hatred of the enemy race.

Only a child's talk, we may say, but the border made
men and women of children overnight, and the boy Lewis
had thrown off childish ways to wage relentless war against
the race which had shown him the pain and terror of the
captive.

Back in the routine of daily work he did not forget. Every idle hour was spent in some occupation that trained him for a hunter of wild animals or wilder men. In a district where every man was a crack shot the deadly aim of Lewis Wetzel became a matter of general knowledge. It is said that he learned to drive a nail with a bullet as far as he could see it. He learned to load a rifle on the run, a trick that few if any other mastered. In a community where most of one's time was spent out of doors and everyone was athletic, Lewis surpassed others in strength and speed. With his mind set on one thing and his body trained to serve it the youth was prepared when opportunity offered to carry out his childish oath.

Life of course was primitive. The first essential was to obtain food and clothing; the next to assure some degree of safety. Education as we think of it now was meager or missing entirely. Lewis' school was the endless forest, his books the demonstrations of untamed nature. In this institution of learning he was an apt pupil, for he mastered the art of woodcraft so well that his proficiency was outstanding, even in a community where all must know something about it.

"One day in June of 1780—Lewis was 16 years old at the time—a party of Indians made an incursion into Pennsylvania, on the headwaters of Wheeling Creek, and stole some horses. Settlers made up a party and followed the raiders down the stream. Arriving opposite the Wetzel place they saw Lewis cultivating corn. They invited the wiry-looking, black-haired boy to join them and help catch the horse thieves.

"This was probably as tempting as an invitation to go fishing would be to a modern boy, but Lewis declined. His father had told him to cultivate corn; he did not like to disobey his father, whom it is said he loved and feared. However, the men insisted, and the boy gave in. Unhitching his father's favorite mare he mounted her and with rifle in hand joined the party in pursuit of the Indians.

"Jogging down the river mile after mile, each minute taking them farther away from home and farther into unknown and perhaps Indian territory, had its cooling effect on the wrath of the robbed settlers. But young Lewis was fresh to the trail. It was good to feel the springy step of the little mare after the tedious plodding between rows of corn and around stumps that dotted the field. How soothing the gentle lope of the horse compared with the unexpected jerk of the handles as the crude cultivator hit a hidden root. How cool the welcome shade after the hot, unprotected cornfield.

"Down to the Ohio River led the hoof marks of the stolen horses. The owners followed, crossed the river and continued on the trail through the hills on the Ohio side until they came to a spring in what is now Belmont County. Here the Indians, believing themselves safe from pursuit, had stopped to rest. They lay down to sleep, allowing the horses to crop the luscious grass that grew near the spring.

"The Whites came suddenly upon the unsuspecting braves as the latter were snoozing in the shade. With bounds like panthers the reds were up and out of sight in the woods, abandoning the stolen horses to any fate.

"This peaceful and happy recovery of their stolen property prompted the settlers to plan their return with confident deliberation. The hasty flight of the redskins had apparently removed all danger from that source. Therefore it was decided to leave the horses which the settlers had ridden, and which were pretty well fagged from the long trip, to rest in the shade while the homeward start would be made with the recaptured steeds. A few men were to remain with the resting horses and follow later when the hard-ridden beasts had somewhat recuperated from the effects of their journey.

"Acting on this plan most of the party set out for home. History does not record the number who stayed to make up the rear guard, nor the manner of their selection, whether they volunteered or were drafted for the job.

When they were ready to depart and were about to approach the horses three Indians suddenly appeared between them and the animals. The surprised Whites did not stop to argue but took to their heels, thus saving their scalps and losing their horses.

"Fear sped their footsteps as they raced from the spring as fast as they had jogged toward it. They overtook the rest of the party and reported the event which had again put the redskins in possession of their property.

"Among the horses abandoned was John Wetzel's favorite mare, which Lewis had so blithely ridden from the cornfield. The thought of this fine animal in the hands of the hated reds, and of the wrath of his father when apprised of the loss, drove young Lewis to disapprove the proceedings.

" 'You couple of dozen empty coonskin caps,' said the boy, or words to that effect. 'You drag me away from my work, let me risk my neck stumbling over rocks and logs and then let three sneaking savages steal my father's best horse. A fine crowd of cowards you turned out to be!'

" 'The boy is right', spoke up a grizzled veteran of the woods, who had insisted that he go along. 'He dropped his duties to help us and it is poor pay we are offering—letting the thieving reds keep his horse. It's a poor showing we are making of ourselves, too, coming all this distance to hand over our horses to the Miamis. We'll be the laughing stock of the Ohio Valley.'

"Other comments were made. The majority had enough Indian chasing and were for getting out of the vicinity as quick as possible, figuring that a whole skin was worth more than a tired horse. But one man sided with the veteran and the two expressed their willingness to go back and get the horses if it were necessary to fight their way through Indians knee deep. With Lewis in the lead the three retraced their steps toward the spring to recover the horses and regain their honor.

" 'When we see the reds we'll tree and fight it out with them,' said Lewis. The others nodded assent. 'Treeing' was the Indian method of warfare, when each man hid behind a tree for protection while scheming how to get at his opponent behind another tree.

"Whites and reds sighted each other at the same time. Lewis 'treed' according to schedule and looked around to see where his supporting friends were. He saw them— several hundred yards to the rear, headed for the river as fast as they could run. Here was a situation worthy the mettle of a Wetzel, and Lewis met it, armed as he was with a skill and cunning equal to that of the most crafty brave who ever roamed the hills.

"Placing his hat over the end of his gun he pushed it out slowly as if he were peeking around the side of the tree. The woods rang with the joint reverberations of three muskets as the deceived warriors blazed away at what they thought was the boy's head. As the hat dropped to the ground the reds dropped their guns and sprang forward to remove the lad's hair. Lewis stepped from his tree and shot the foremost Indian through the breast.

"The two others, thinking the boy helpless with his gun empty, came on brandishing tomahawks and shouting in glee. But again they reckoned without the Wetzel resourcefulness. Springing away like a deer the boy easily kept out of their reach. Meanwhile he was loading his gun as he ran. With a breech-loading rifle this is no great feat, but a muzzle-loader is different. Anyone who has measured the powder and poured it down a long barrel standing still knows it requires a steady hand. Placing the wadding and tamping it down with the long ramrod and then fitting the bullet to the muzzle and driving it home is harder to do than to describe and takes more time. Then priming the flintlock without spilling all the powder out of the pan is another test for steady nerves. But young Lewis accomplished this difficult and delicate operation while on the dead run. With his gun again loaded he turned suddenly and coolly put an end to another pursuer.

"The third Indian, astonished at this trick, hesitated a second, then came on with renewed speed, hoping to catch the lad before he could load again. Wetzel's speed blighted this hope, and for the second time the White whose 'gun was always loaded' turned and made another squaw a widow.

"Collecting his three scalps and his horse the victor joined his companions, remarking that he would rather re-

Wetzel's Spring at St. Clairsville as it is now

turn without his scalp and with the mare than without the mare but with his hair."[29]

The spring where the youthful Wetzel killed his first Indian is still known as Wetzel's Spring, and may be seen by the inquisitive traveler who journeys to St. Clairsville, Ohio, and asks about it.

The episode of the stolen horses brought Lewis into prominence throughout the region, where daring was held

---

29. W. Scott Powell's "History of Marshall County."

in high regard and skill in Indian warfare was a useful accomplishment. The boy with three scalps and all the glory stood out from the others of the party, none of whom had taken a scalp or showed any unusual degree of courage. It enhanced the youth's reputation so much that when the general assembly wanted a scout to protect that part of the country Lewis got the job. It was exactly to his liking. Shouldering his gun and bidding his folks a brief farewell he set out through the shadows of the forest, bent on getting an Indian wherever and whenever he could find one. In fact his enthusiasm for this sport got him in trouble with white authorities more than once.

No scruples hampered his efficiency and no sympathy stayed his hand when a red victim was in sight. Without mercy, and expecting none, he sought and slew the reds as an occupation, becoming the hero of the hour by doing it.

We may marvel that such heartless behavior would be tolerated let alone acclaimed by so-called civilized white associates who inhabited the settlements and administered what little law was in effect, but a glimpse at the times may explain it.

The noble red man of the forest was not exactly a nice neighbor, especially as he watched his white neighbors taking his land and killing the game which was his food and clothing. He had plenty of faults, and they were not reduced by contact with civilization. The combination of a revengeful spirit, bad whiskey, cheating traders and grasping settlers brought out the worst in his nature. His cruelty might find its mark on animal as well as on man.

"One day Indians stole some 20 horses from settlers near Wheeling and hamstrung the animals. To put them out of their suffering the beasts had to be killed. About this time—it was in the year 1781—a man with his tongue torn from his mouth and both hands cut off reached the settlement. He could neither talk nor write, but words or letters were unnecessary to explain his misery. The man did not live long, but the memory of his suffering dwelt in the minds of the Whites, fanning the fire of public hatred against the Indians. A scout sleeping in a hollow tree one night heard a terrific explosion. On investigation the next morning he found six dead Indians and the body of a white woman. She had been captured and made the wife of a chief. To get revenge for her treatment she threw a bag of powder into the campfire, killing herself and all the Indians. Her death recruited more scouts and created new thirst for blood along the frontier."[30]

---

30. R. C. V. Myers, *"Wetzel the Scout."*

CHAPTER IV

The Position That Pointed to Lewis' Life Work

THE Revolutionary War was still raging. Indians often led a party of redcoats through grain fields, tramping down the crop. They would go to houses, take the food, capture or kill the father and leave the woman and children facing starvation or the mercy of neighbors. Simon Girty, renegade White of black reputation, was indulging in a savagery which added to the horrors of the frontier.

After a night of devastation the settlers became so wrought up over the continued danger that an assembly was held at Wheeling to name scouts to help protect their homes. The services of these scouts were to be voluntary, even their supplies to be furnished by themselves. All the pay they got out of it was the pleasure, if any, of hunting Indians and the satisfaction of serving their fellow men. It was this dangerous and wageless job that Lewis Wetzel landed, after much pleading. He was considered too young, but he convinced the assembly that he was old in experience and cunning.

At the age of 17 Wetzel may be said to have entered on his life work, that of hunting Indians. The warfare with the reds was not restrained by proclamations or politicians. It was a free fight. Anybody could enter and keep at it as long as he liked. The rules were simple and consisted of "Get his scalp".

Wetzel was a stern, sober, silent sort of person, never boasting of his exploits, but pursuing his way with a tenacity which made his name as much feared by the foe as they were hated by him. He shunned the company of other people and was never so content as when roaming the forests like a wild animal.

Wetzel's picturesque appearance joined with his growing reputation for daring added to his popularity with border folks. Five feet ten inches tall, unusually strong and well developed in arms and shoulders, slight and active of limb, with piercing black eyes, scowling brow and black hair which when combed out hung to his knees, this ranger was the object of much approval on the part of the young ladies at the settlements. Graceful, morose, fascinating and blind to their charms the dashing youth doubtless wreaked considerable havoc among the feminine hearts not recorded by tradition or listed in printed tales of the frontier. His true love was the long trail and the thrill of encounter. Like a knight of old he had dedicated his life to decimating the heathen, and he was not to be wafted from his course by the wiles of backwoods belles.

But the hand that held the rifle in deadly aim and the ear that caught the faintest whisper of wind-stirred leaves could do more than speed the whining bullet or detect the muffled tread of skulking warrior. For Wetzel was a musician—of sorts. He played the fiddle.

There is something eminently fitting in the thought of this half-tamed son of the wilderness pouring out his wild soul through the strains of the trembling violin string, telling things his stumbling tongue could not put forth in words.

When hardy plowmen in cowhide boots and husky axemen in deerskin shirts stepped out on the puncheon floor with laughing girls in homespun dress it was young Lewis who mounted an empty whiskey barrel and put the spirit of dancing sunbeans or gurgling streams into willing feet.

Although Wetzel has long been laid to rest and his fiddle is now none knows where, the old tunes linger still. In the shelter of the mountains, when long shadows announce the night, these immortals emerge from hidden dell and frowning hill. . . . With a cadence and a tempo and a lilt

that cannot be caught they give way to wild abandon in
a language of their own.   All the longing and the striving
and the hope and pain and fear, all the joy and bold ad-
vances, all the confidence of youth, with the spirit of the
forests and the freedom of the plain they depict.   These
old tunes, in their elusive fantasy, recall a mighty epoch
in local history.   When captured by musicians and trans-
ferred to notes on paper they are like wild animals in a
cage.   They are not the same.   The skill of a Kreisler may
tempt them from retreat, but only the man of the mountains
who knows their ways and has their confidence can make
them perform in natural fashion.   The jazz-hound misses
them entirely, and even the careful and sympathetic student
admits his defeat.   For a hundred years and more these
haunting strains have dwelt in the Appalachians, defying
the inroads of progress and smiling on the favored few
who by tradition and temperament are their worthy heirs.

Thus the one social grace of young Wetzel stamps him
as a man of attainment and importance in spite of the array of evidence that would picture him a near felon.   No
common killer was this long-haired hunter, but a man with
a mission, a soul of determination imbued with a single
great idea, mistaken as it may have been, a product of his
times and a victim of false values.

Uncouth, uneducated, ill at ease in company, yet nursing
a fierce pride and presenting a haughty demeanor to hide
his feeling of inferiority when in the presence of more
polished people, inured to danger and excelling in popular
feats of strength and physical skill, we can readily believe
that he was a great temptation to the ladies and might have
shone as a master of ceremonies or even a movie hero if
living to-day.   However, his dark, pock-marked face and
morose disposition might have landed him in some such
honorable occupation as a college professor or a truck
driver.   He received no "mash notes".   Girls were more
direct—or circumspect—those days.   They came to the

point without preliminaries.   Along with the Indians they found him too slippery an individual to catch.

Little Bertha Rosencranz liked him pretty well.   She was a friend of the family and if she had slapped his face for his rudeness instead of pitying him for his wounds the history of the Ohio Valley might have been vastly different. For there is no question of his influence in making the section uncomfortably hot for the redskins and hence safer for the Whites.   With a wife depending on him it is pretty certain that he would have been less keen to risk his neck chasing reds.   But if Napoleon had won the battle of Waterloo or George Washington had been born a Turk, history might have been different too.   We get nowhere by these idle suppositions.   But Bertha thought the strong hunter would be handy to have around the cabin, winning all the turkey shoots and bringing in a deer every time the ice-box got empty.

CHAPTER V

BORDER STANDARDS AS SHOWN THROUGH EXPERIENCES OF DIFFERENT INDIVIDUALS

(1) *Martin, Lewis' Brother*

LEWIS' aversion to redskins was felt by his brother Martin. While the former excelled as a marksman the latter surpassed in skill with the tomahawk. Martin's mastery of this weapon brought him into prominence, and sometimes trouble, more than once. Aside from his hatred of Indians he is said to have been a genial companion, a true friend, and a trusted citizen.

At the age of 20 we find Martin Wetzel[31] a soldier under Major Samuel McColloch, the man who is said to have jumped his horse over the precipitous Wheeling hill to escape the Indians.

In September, 1777, when danger from the Indians was suspected to the settlers of the flats of Grave Creek, now Moundsville, W. Va., and Colonel David Shepherd sent out Captain William Foreman with a company of men to the relief of the Grave Creek settlers, Martin Wetzel was one of that company. Captain Foreman and his men reached the flats of Grave Creek, now Moundsville, W. Va. Finding everything safe from the Indians there they started to return to the fort at Wheeling. When about five miles north of what is now Moundsville, in the north end of the narrows

---

31. Martin Wetzel and his father, Captain John Wetzel, and Lewis Bonnett, a brother-in-law of Captain John Wetzel, were in the battle of Point Pleasant under General Andrew Lewis, Oct. 10, 1774. Martin Wetzel was only 17 years old at that time. Lewis Bonnett to Lyman C. Draper, *Draper's Mss.* 11E132 and 2E8, in the State Historical Society of Wisconsin, Madison, Wisconsin.

where McMechen, W. Va., is now located, things became suspicious when the soldiers found some Indian beads and trinkets scattered along the path. Martin Wetzel then a boy past 20 years old urged Captain Foreman to go over the hill instead of around the Ohio river bank where the Indian trinkets were scattered for a bait.

Captain Foreman's Grave as it appeared in 1790.
(Courtesy, J. H. Branter, Sr.)

The Captain laughed and said that he didn't need the advice of a 20-year-old boy in regard to Indian warfare. However, Martin Wetzel and a few other soldiers did take the path over the hill against Captain Foreman's orders. Captain Foreman and 21 of his men continued to follow the path along the bank of the Ohio River. A short distance from where they found the Indian trinkets, while marching along in perfect safety they thought, the savages poured a deadly volley of bullets from behind the trees. Captain Foreman and 21 of his brave men fell dead. Martin Wetzel and his few men were directly above the savages on the hill, hearing the noise of the Indian guns they all fired and yelled at the top of their voices. The Indians thinking they were being attacked from the rear by a large army, ran.

Martin Wetzel and his few men returned safe to the fort at Wheeling. The next day Colonel Shepherd sent a crew of men from the fort at Wheeling to bury Captain Foreman and his men. Martin Wetzel was one of the crew to help bury those unfortunate soldiers. They were all buried in one grave in a little ravine near the Ohio River.[32] Pawpaw bark was stripped to handle the bodies while burying them.

In 1780 Martin Wetzel was one of 400 men in Colonel Brodhead's army that set out on an expecition against the Indian towns on the Coshocton River.[33] "There is no place for an Indian but what a bullet gives him," said the boy Martin Wetzel as the march from Wheeling started. This sentiment was apparently shared by the rest of the party, judging from the outcome of the expedition.

The command reached the Indian village,[34] surrounded one and captured every man, woman and child in it, without firing a shot. One would think that this easy victory would make the victors magnanimous, but the milk of human kindness had evidently turned sour in their fierce breasts.

---

32. Captain Foreman and his men's bones were later removed to Mt. Rose cemetery, Moundsville, W. Va., where they now lie.

33. Lewis Bonnett, an uncle of Martin Wetzel, and Martin Wetzel were spies in this campaign. Lewis Wetzel was not in this expedition. Martin was in Kentucky but returned in time to go along. Bonnett to Draper, *Draper's Mss.* 11E92, in the State Historical Society of Wisconsin, Madison, Wisconsin.

34. They proceeded as far as the White Eye Plains and returned. This was also called the White Women's Expedition. Bonnett to Draper, *Draper's Mss.* 11E94, in the State Historical Society of Wisconsin, Madison, Wisconsin.

Sixteen warriors were made prisoners in the raid. A council was held to determine their fate. The verdict was death. This was carried out, each brave being bound, dispatched with tomahawk and scalped. Martin Wetzel's tomahawk was the first one raised against the helpless prisoners.

Another nice trick to the discredit of this "army" occurred the next morning when an Indian appeared on the opposite bank of the river and asked for the "big Captain". When Colonel Brodhead asked the Indian what he wanted the man replied, "I want peace."

"Send over some of your chiefs," said Brodhead.

"Maybe you kill," replied the peacemaker.

"They shall not be killed," promised the colonel.

Accordingly one of the chiefs paddled across the river and started talking with the colonel. Martin Wetzel, tomahawk hidden under his hunting shirt, crept unnoticed behind the chief and buried his weapon in the redman's skull. For this treacherous assault Martin received no punishment. The sentiment in the so-called army approved the deed so strongly that the commander was unable to mete out justice.

On the return 20 prisoners were entrusted to their tender care. A few squaws and children lived to reach Fort Pitt, but the remainder were slaughtered in a march of murder with the swift tomahawk of Martin Wetzel much in evidence in the slaughter.[35]

Yet this "congenial companion and true friend" was

---

35. This story, and the one of prisoners killed as related before, is the customary account of the event, but its historical accuracy has been questioned. Hassler in his *"Old Westmoreland"* intimates that it may have originated from "exaggerated yarns told by ignorant frontiersmen, beside log cabin fires, into the ears of the wondering boy" (Joseph Doddridge, author of *"Notes on the Settlement and Indian Wars of Virginia and Pennsylvania"*). "Martin Wetzel and William Morgan, noted frontier scouts, had narrow escapes from the Indians at Kingwood, Preston County, West Virginia, during the Indian raids there from 1778 to 1788." Booklet, 1938—*West Virginia Highway Marker*.

respected on the border. He must have possessed some redeeming qualities, but history fails to record them. So confused were the historians and so saturated with fear the settlers that the will to kill redskins was the highest recommendation they thought necessary.

We are left a list of similar episodes, all proving that the attitude of Martin Wetzel, when Indians were the victims, did not change with years.

It is futile for us to measure the past in standards of the present. We look with horror on the wholesale killing in pioneer times, failing to justify the actions of government or the views of the people. But who knows how our descendants a century hence will regard us? What will they think, for instance, of the tens of thousands of lives lost annually under the wheels of speeding motor cars? What will they say of our social and industrial system that throws aside the aged as useless, permits unemployment, hardship and want?

On these grounds we may apologize for the acts of our predecessors, but on humanitarian grounds we search in vain for alibis. Their lives were hard and their manners rough. Weakness was akin to failure, and failure meant death. They lived close to nature, and nature in spite of her beautiful dress and cheerful moods is relentless, cruel and no friend of the underdog. A salmon lays ten million eggs but only two live to be salmon. Tender grasses are smothered by tough weeds. A constant struggle, from ant to elephant, from violet to oak tree, and woe betide the one who stumbles. His "name is Dennis", and his throne is mud.

In a life story of Wetzel and other border heroes, written by Cecil B. Hartley in 1860, the author says: "The character and actions of these men will form a profitable study for the patriotic young men, who may be called upon to defend the homes and firesides of our country; and they will not fail to inspire that noble and generous emulation which has always formed a striking trait in the American character".

DeHass, chronicler of the early settlement and Indian wars of western Virginia, says, "The memory of Wetzel should be embalmed in the hearts of the people of western Virginia, for his efforts in defense of their forefathers are without parallel in border warfare".

By others, however, Wetzel was regarded as little better than a half-savage, a man with a tiger disposition and a blood-thirsty spirit.

"Some years after the Coshocton holocaust Martin Wetzel and a man named Wolf were captured by the Indians on the south fork of Wheeling Creek near Ryerson's Fork, and about two miles above where Ryerson's Station was erected a few years afterwards. They had been sent from Wheeling Fort to some of the forts on the Monongahela as spies. According to his own statement, there were eighteen guns fired at him, and five of them at not more than 25 yards. One bullet made a streak across his hip bone, and another along his side. It is likely that the party that had him did not know of his record with Colonel Brodhead for they did not put an end to him at once but took him along with them. Out across Ohio they trudged, going north, until they reached a village in the northern part of the state.

"When captives sulked or lagged they usually put an end to them at once but when they were cheerful the captors frequently kept and adopted them. Martin, knowing this, saved his life by exhibiting a cheerful contentment which so thoroughly deceived the Indians that the first that caught him, adopted him into his family and Martin was admitted to their council assembly, but his revengeful spirit only waxed stronger during his year in the tepee with the reds. Wolf was tortured and burned to death.

"His chance came in the fall of the year when three young chiefs took him with them on a hunting trip. He did the cooking and made it his custom to be the first back to camp after a day's hunt. One evening he met one of the hunters alone and proceeded to show the brave some tricks with the rifle that his father had taught him. The red man turned his head, being off guard, and Wetzel shot him in the breast. Scalping this victim he threw the body in a hole made by an uprooted tree and covered it with brush. Back in camp he pretended to be anxious about his victim, but his companions laughingly refused to be alarmed, saying that the absent one could take care of himself.

"The next morning Martin cautiously followed the other two as they started to hunt. All day long he kept to their trail. As night approached he strode up to them and detained one while the other walked on. With a sweep of the merciless tomahawk the white man split the red man's head. Another 'good' Indian, and the pleased White trotted back to camp in time to meet the remaining warrior as he staggered in under a load of game. Martin offered to relieve him of the burden. As the red stooped to unload, the tomahawk fell again, and Martin Wetzel's vengeance was complete. Free from danger of pursuit and with three scalps to prove his prowess the escaped White proceeded to the nearest settlement.

"He told them that the Indians would steal their horses and were planning an attack on them. They told Martin he was a spy and only wanted to drag them out in order to be massacred by the Indians. One of the men took a well loaded rifle and snapped it at Martin's breast, but the gun happened to miss fire. Martin then told them to send for Colonel Daniel Boone and in case Boone said he was a spy, they might shoot him. He was held as a prisoner until Boone was brought in, who told them that he was acquainted with Wetzel and had fought with him three years before, and told them at what places. Wetzel was released and Boone took him home with him, and in the fall of the same year Martin came home to Wheeling."[36]

---

36. Lewis Bonnett to Draper, Nov. 8, 1846, *Draper's Mss.* 11E93, in the State Historical Society of Wisconsin, Madison, Wisconsin.

The technique of this enterprise throws some light on border standards. If Martin Wetzel had simply run away from the Indians, as he could easily have done during his year with them, the fact would have been forgotten with the numerous other similar escapes; but that he bided his time and killed three Indians was that extra flourish so approved by the settlers that the account has come down to us with all its gruesome details.

The following narrative is exactly as Lewis Bonnett, Jr., wrote Lyman C. Draper on January 24, 1849.

"In the month of May, 1791, in the same year as St. Clairs' defeat, the Indians took horses belonging to my father, Lewis Bonnett, Sr.; one belonging to Henry Winters, and a bay mare belonging to Martin Wetzel. It was on Saturday night and there was a muster or training of the militia that day. My father was captain, and he was one of the first militia captains in Ohio county which embraced Brooke, Marshall, Tyler, Wetzel and Wood counties. Martin Wetzel and Henry Winters lodged at my father's house that night, sitting up late and talking, by which means the Indians discovered there were several men in the house. Otherwise they probably would have attacked and murdered the whole family, which were in number, father, mother, three sisters, myself and brother.

"The next morning as soon as it was discovered that the horses were gone, word was carried through the neighborhood. My father began to make buckskin moccasins. My mother and sisters were engaged in making biscuits. About ten o'clock on the same day (Sunday) there were nine men that made their appearance equipped for the pursuit of the party of Indians that stole the horses. They took the trail and crossed the river that evening, and followed the trail to within nine miles of their town where the Indians had made a halt. They had killed a deer and were making saddles of moss and platting them with bark when the party came upon them.

"Only three Indians could be seen. One was sitting on our horse. One was standing on the opposite side of the horse from the party, and one was roasting meat at the fire. It was agreed that three should shoot. William McColloch was to shoot the one on our horse, who was leaning forward tying his stirrup. Martin Wetzel was to shoot the one standing on the opposite side of the horse, and Thomas Boggs was to shoot the one roasting meat. Boggs and Wetzel killed theirs on the spot. McColloch made a good shot but the Indian fell hanging in the stirrups; as the bullet hit him in the side. He finally got loose from the stirrups and made his way off into the bushes. He did not get more than a half-mile away before he died. His wound bled profusely and some of the party wanted to follow the bloody trail, but my father told them there was no use as they had the horses back, and besides he might be hiding behind a log waiting to shoot them, and that it would be better to make a hasty retreat lest they might be pursued.

"The party took his advice and did not follow the wounded Indian, but got their two scalps and their horses and returned home safely."[37]

"When the Indians are gone the land will be ours, and the sooner they are killed the better," was the blunt way one settler soldier expressed it. Mercy on the part of the Whites usually got them in trouble with their own people. When Colonel David Williamson turned a bunch of harmless captives, who had no crime against them, over to the commander of Fort Pitt, and the latter later released them, public disapproval was so strong that Williamson was in disgrace. So thoroughly was he disliked that he later perpetrated the Gnadenhutten massacre of Moravian Indians,[38]

37. Bonnett to Draper, *Draper's Mss.* 11E84 and 11E90. in the State Historical Society of Wisconsin, Madison, Wisconsin.
38. "My father, Lewis Bonnett, was in Colonel Williamson's Moravian campaign, but he took no part in murdering the four inoffensive Indians. Martin Wetzel was along. My father moved back to Wheeling Creek that same year." Lewis Bonnett to Draper, *Draper's Mss.* 11E27 and 11E28, in the State Historical Society of Wisconsin, Madison, Wisconsin.

Ebenezer Zane's Cabin near Fort Henry from which Betty Zane carried the powder, and he defended during the second seige. (Courtesy, The Wheeling News-Register)

for which the redskins paid by burning Colonel Crawford at the stake.

(2) Betty Zane

But this was war. Not a nice civilized war, with uniforms, music and colors flying, but a war to the finish conducted according to the style of the times and the rules of the enemy. And the men were not the only heroes. It took little Betty Zane to show them at Wheeling that a pioneer girl had as much bravery and enterprise as the best of them, for when Fort Henry was surrounded by howling savages and the defenders' powder ran low, it is said she scurried across the arrow-swept "no-man's-land" to Ebenezer Zane's house and returned with her apron full of powder to save the day.

Lewis Wetzel was present at the Fort Henry affair, at Wheeling in 1782, and it is said that his unerring aim accounted for his share of attackers, but he was not the center of the stage, as he was at Fort Beeler in the same year.

(3) Attacks on Fort Henry

Fort Fincastle was later changed to Fort Henry and stood at Wheeling, Va., now West Virginia. It was built in 1774. The Indians attacked this fort twice. The first attack was on September 1, 1777, when a large body of Indians and British soldiers under a White leader appeared before the fort and asked that it surrender and be taken to Detroit and accept the terms of Governor Hamilton. The thirty-three men in the fort refused to surrender and resolved to hold it or die in its defense. The women assisted by taking their places alongside of the men and fought just as bravely and effectively as the men. Among the defenders of the fort at this siege were: Colonel David Shepherd, who was in command of the fort, and his son William Shepherd, Major Samuel McColloch, Colonel Andrew Swearingen, Martin Wetzel, Samuel, James, and Joseph Tomlin-

Fort Henry at Wheeling.   (Courtesy of The Wheeling News-Register)

son, Ebenezer, Andrew, Silas, and Jonathan Zane, Dr. James and William McMechen, Abraham Rogers, Joseph Biggs, Bazel Duke, Robert Lemon, John Lynn and John Caldwell.   There were fifteen killed and nine wounded belonging to the fort. It is not known how many Indians and British were killed and wounded but they gave up the siege and left the vicinity after burning all the cabins and driving off all the livestock that they could find.

The second Indian attack on Fort Henry was on September 11, 1782, and is known as the last battle of the Revolutionary War.   There were forty British soldiers under Captain Pratt and 260 Indians under George Girty; also Joseph Brant, a notorious Tory and Matthew Elliott aided the British and Indians in this attack. Silas Zane was in command of the fort during this siege in the absence of Captain John Boggs. The fort had about twenty men and several women to fight against this large army. Colonel Ebenezer Zane with his Negro slave, Sam, and his wife, Kate, remained to defend his own cabin. Some of the defenders of the fort were: Lewis and Martin Wetzel, Moses Shepherd, Daniel Sullivan, John Lynn, Andrew Scott, George Greer, a man named Tate, Captain John Wetzel, Andrew and Jonathan Zane; Betty Zane, Lydia Boggs, and Molly Scott were among the women of the fort who rendered invaluable service in saving it from its invaders.[39]

After several days and nights the Indians and the British again gave up the siege and left the vicinity after again burning all the buildings and taking all the livestock in the vicinity. This was one of the most important battles fought between the Indians and the Whites along the frontier and ranks next in importance to the Battle of Point Pleasant which was fought October 10, 1774. It is said that Lewis Wetzel shot the first Indian in this attack as he rode toward the fort, and that Martin and Lewis Wetzel stood cool as cucumbers on the platform by the portholes

---

39. See footnotes 111 and 112.

Battle of Fort Henry

(Courtesy, The Wheeling News-Register)

picking the redskins off as they came within gunshot. Only one inmate of the fort was wounded during this attack and none were killed, but a large number of Indians and several British were killed and wounded. This was the last time that the British flag was flown in battle in the Revolutionary War.

(4) Attack at Beeler Station

About 1782 Shawnee and Mohawk Indians attacked Fort Beeler in what is now Marshall County, W. Va. Martin

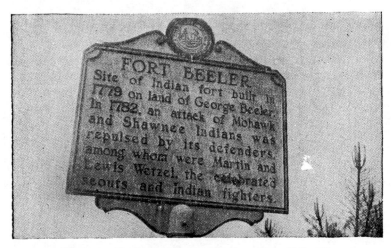

Highway Marker at Beeler Station along U.S. 250.

Wetzel and a man named Younkins had been made scouts for the fort. Lewis ran across them and accompanied them to the fort. Colonel Beeler expected an attack and was prepared in everything except man power. He needed more men, a rather common need in war time.

Two chiefs rode toward the fort side by side. They stopped to dismount, when a rifle cracked and one of them fell dead. It was Lewis Wetzel's reply to intended negotiations. Himself safe behind the walls he again played the game according to the simple rules he knew.

The Indians were furious and stormed the place. They tried to dig under the walls. Martin and Lewis saw the dirt moving and watched it carefully. Presently a plumed head appeared and the owner tried to squeeze through. Martin helped him, by sinking his tomahawk in the scalp lock and dragging the dead red up through the hole he had dug. The second Indian, thinking the first safe inside the fort, stuck his head through the hole, to be met with the same reception at the hands of Lewis.

The Wetzels defending Fort Beeler

In this manner six Indians were killed, drawn into the fort and thrown aside. The seventh, becoming suspicious, peeped before trying to crawl in and saw the Wetzels waiting with tomahawks in hand. He dodged back, but Lewis struck at him, wounding him in the shoulder. He ran away. This ended the Indians' attempt to dig under the fort.

Outside the redskins howled like a pack of hungry wolves, or watched in a silence worse than warwhoops, for

it meant that they were planning new modes of attack.
Colonel Beeler's little force was too small to cope with them.
As a solution for this unpleasant predicament the Wetzel
brothers suggested that the women and children make dummies and place them with rifles at the portholes. When this
was done the Indians blazed away at the dummies, wasting
their ammunition and deciding that the defending force
was much larger than it really was. After a day and a
night they retreated.

During this attack on Fort Beeler the Indians secured
a big hollow log and filled it partly full of powder and ball.
They aimed it at the gate of the fort, thinking it would
make a good cannon, and touched it off. It exploded, killing seven Indians and wounding five.

(5) John Wetzel, Jr.

John Wetzel, Jr., also had his share of encounters with
the redskins. When only sixteen years old, with Abraham
Earliwine in search of a mare and colt which had strayed,
he was ambushed and captured. Indians seeing the mare,
which had a bell on, removed the bell and tied it to one of
their wrists. The boys followed the sound of the bell and
walked into the Indians' trap. Four redmen caught and
bound them, John getting shot through the arm in the
fracas. On their march to the Ohio, Earliwine complained
so much that the captors tomahawked him.

Reaching the Ohio river near the mouth of Grave
Creek,[40] the redmen found some hogs, killed one and put
it in a canoe they had stolen. Three of the Indians with
the captive, wounded boy and the dead hog got in the canoe,
while the fourth red swam their horses as they crossed the
stream.

That very morning Isaac Williams, Hamilton Carr,
William McColloch, and a Dutchman named Jacob came
down from Wheeling to the deserted settlement at the
mouth of the creek to look after the livestock left there.

---

40. Near where Moundsville, W. Va., now stands.

They heard the report of the rifle when the Indians shot the hog. Hurrying on they spotted the canoe in midstream. McColloch jumped up on the bank and shot one of the Indians in the canoe and he fell dead into the river. Williams shot another Indian and he fell into the water but holding on to the side of the canoe with a death grip. John Wetzel, lying in the bottom of the craft, wounded, yelled out, "Don't shoot me. I am a white man."

Spot on the Ohio River where John Wetzel was rescued at the mouth of Grave Creek.

McColloch said, "John Wetzel, is that you?" The answer was, "Yes".

"Paddle to shore," replied McColloch.

John answered, "No paddle in the canoe."

"Paddle with your hands," yelled McColloch.

"I am wounded," said John.

"Knock that Indian loose and swim to shore," McColloch answered.

John picked up a tomahawk that was in the canoe, split the Indian's head and cut off his fingers holding the canoe and let him sink into the river. He then got out of the canoe and swam to the shore with the aid of one hand. Carr and the Dutchman Jacob, both shot at the Indian that was swimming the horses across the river but he was too far away to hurt. The third Indian that was in the canoe jumped out and started to swim, but McColloch, who soon had his gun reloaded, shot him before he got out of gun shot and he sank to the bottom of the Ohio river.

The canoe was turned adrift and was later retrieved near Maysville, Kentucky, the dead hog which had been the means of saving the boy's life still in it.[39]

"As a boy John Wetzel witnessed a forest tragedy which left an impression on him all his life. He found a little papoose lying on the ground in its birchbark box. The grave-eyed infant was so interesting that John thought it a good idea to steal the child. So he picked it up and carried it out of the woods. At the edge of the forest he was confronted by a squaw who held out her arms and said, "Mine. Squaw followed white boy with papoose out of woods". John handed the baby to the woman and was horrified to see her dash it to the ground, killing it.

Just then another squaw dashed up, distraught and wild. "My papoose", she cried.

From charges, counter charges, admission and threats of the one furious and the other defiant woman, John learned that jealousy over the child's father had caused the woman to commit the fiendish act. She was so desperate that she urged the infant's mother to kill her, but the latter with a fine appreciation of a greater punishment said, "Live! If you kill to punish those you love, then live."

The grief of the mother held the boy in a spell as the destroyer moved into the forest. Then the full import of the tragedy breaking on him, the lad turned with a wild cry of fear and fled from the spot.

    41. This episode happened in June, 1786. Bonnett to Draper, *Draper's Mss.* 11E88 and 11E89 in the State Historical Society of Wisconsin, Madison, Wisconsin.

"In later years, John Jr., did his part in discouraging the Indians' habit of stealing horses. One time he led a party, composed of Thomas Boggs, Joseph Hedges, John Linn, John McColloch, Kinzie Dickerson, and his brother Jacob Wetzel, against an Indian town on the headwaters of Still Water or some of the branches of Wiles Creek. It was in the fall of 1789 or 1790. The party wanted to get revenge on the reds for taking horses from the settlers. They found the horses which they secured without opposition, for not a redskin showed up to confront the angry owners. The Whites knew the reds would follow, so made all possible haste, but on the second day of the trip back, Linn was taken violently sick. The party halted and guarded their back trail. Just before dawn a guard went to dip some water from a stream and noticed that it was muddy. This indicated that Indians were walking down the stream from above, and served to warn the Whites. Hearing nothing they concluded it might be raccoons wading in the water, so lay down again, but on the alert.

The campfire burned low and the enemy stole silently down the stream, reaching within ten or a dozen feet of the Whites without discovery. The reds fired, killing the sick man, Linn, and followed up by attacking the others. Hedges was killed outright and Boggs was shot through the thigh, but he defended himself to the very last. When a party returned the next day to bury the dead, they found that Boggs' fingernails were all black. He had been tomahawked to pieces by the Indians; as he could not escape because of his broken thigh. McColloch jumped in a quagmire and fooled the Indians into thinking he was dead. The next day he encountered Jacob Wetzel and the two made their way back to Wheeling.

John Wetzel, Jr., ran about nine miles barefooted through the snow, because he did not have time to put on his moccasins. He and Kinzie Dickerson hid in the underbrush where they remained all day and all the next night. The Indians drove the horses over the vicinity to trample the Whites, if any should be hiding; fortunately John and Kinzie escaped this search and finally reached Wheeling."[42-43]

"In 1789 or 1790 there was a contemplated project in progress to raise a sufficient force to demolish the Sandusky towns; as the Indians from those towns were a great pest to the white settlers. Before the plan was put into action, it was necessary to get a common knowledge of the enemy's country; such as the situation of their towns and in order to do this they wanted to get contributions of a large sum to offer two or three who would undertake the hazardous journey. There were $90.00 in money collected besides some other contributions.

"John Wetzel, Jr., Peter Crow, and George McColloch offered their services and made their way to the Sandusky towns. When near the towns they lay in ambush and waited for darkness. During the night they marched right through the middle of the town. They were halted by a dog. An Indian came out of his wigwam and saw them. He instantly gave an alarm. The three brave scouts had no time to lose and made their way back nine or ten miles as fast as possible. The Indians trailed them by the help of their dogs. At last the scouts concluded that they were out of danger, but to their surprise, after they had concealed themselves on a rising knoll in the woods full of bushes, and when they had settled down to remain all day, they were hailed again by an Indian dog. They knew their doom was near and all three made a vow never to surrender, but to fight to the last; knowing if they were captured the Indians would torture them to death at the stake.

"They all three primed their guns, the dogs barking

    42. Lewis Bonnett to Lyman C. Draper, *Draper's Mss.* 11E22 and 11E94 in the State Historical Society of Wisconsin, Madison, Wisconsin.
    43. Lewis Bonnett said that he heard Jacob Wetzel give his brother John, Jr., a complete reprimand for his unguarded and imprudent conduct in this affair. The sun melting the snow the next day saved them from freezing to death and also kept the Indians from tracking and locating them. Bonnett to Draper, *Draper's Mss.* 11E30 in the State Historical Society of Wisconsin, Madison, Wisconsin.

at them all the time. They were keeping a sharp lookout and at length they saw a large Indian creeping towards the barking dogs. They drew lots immediately on who should shoot first. The lot fell on John Wetzel, Jr. The Indian made his way to a tree about forty yards off and peeped out from behind it in the direction of the log behind which the three scouts were hiding. John Wetzel, Jr., took a deliberate aim at the Indian's head. The ball struck him fair between the eyebrows, and John remarked, 'that was his last sickness,' as he fell lifeless to the ground. As soon as the report of Wetzel's rifle was heard there was tremendous yelling round the rising land they were on. John soon reloaded his gun saying to his comrades, 'We must get out of here'. They ran in the direction of which there was no yelling, but were soon confronted by three Indians with uplifted tomahawks. John was in front and never halted but rushed on and the Indians stood their ground. John said in a low voice, 'Peter, shoot the right one; George, shoot the left one, and I will shoot the middle one'. All three fired at the same time and all three Indians fell. They soon reloaded and killed the dogs.

"When cousin John Wetzel, Jr., returned to my father's home, my sister combed the vermin out of his hair with a fine comb and it was full of them. John Wetzel, Jr., had the sole command and the other two were under his control.

"Captain Samuel Brady was a married man at this time, and had a large farm on Short Creek. No married men went into such expeditions. Had he been a member, he certainly would have taken command.

"Jeremiah Williamson lived one and a half miles below David Shepherd's. He went hunting one day on the south side of Shepherd's fort. He hung his shot pouch and powder horn on a bush; stepped back a few paces and shot at it, putting a bullet hole through the pouch and horn. He then put it on and made his way with all speed to the fort, and reported that the Indians had shot at him; producing the shot pouch and powder horn as evidence. A party soon went to investigate; taking Williamson along. He at first sternly refused to go, but some of the party said he must go and show them where the Indians shot at him, as they were suspicious of his story. When he showed them the spot no traces of Indians could be found, and some of the party accused him of shooting the pouch and horn himself. After close questioning by the party, he admitted that he had. When he was asked what he did it for he replied, 'To create some interest and excitement'. Is it likely that John Wetzel, Jr., would take such an unreliable man with him on such a hazardous trip as marching through the Sandusky town in the dead of the night?"[44]

John Wetzel, Jr., and Veach Dickerson painted their bodies and clothed themselves as Indians to go on an Indian scouting trip for adventure and pleasure. "We are half Indian anyway," they remarked, relying on their fluency in the Indian tongue to help them out of any tight places they might enter.

Near the head of the Sandusky river they approached an Indian village, entered it as Indians, but, noting that the inhabitants suspected them, left the next morning and hid along a path. During the day several Indians passed close by, but the watchers only waited. On the evening of the second day two Indians came down the path and the disguised whites stepped out in front of them. The keen eyes of the reds noted something wrong and said, "White man; no like Injuns." Their disguise pierced, the Whites threw aside pretense and John, Jr., knocked down one of the redskins with his tomahawk. Dickerson grappled with the other. Wetzel came to his aid and they bound and gagged the redman.

Scalping the dead one the two captors set off with their prize toward home, taking care to hide their trail by taking a crooked course and keeping on the hardest ground. When they crossed the Muskingum River their prisoner balked.

44. Bonnett to Draper, *Draper's Mss.*, 11E100 and 11E101 in the State Historical Society of Wisconsin, Madison, Wisconsin.

"Indian no go with white cowards," said he.   "Indian rather die by white hands.   Indian brave and free.   Cords make Indian no prisoner."

In spite of all persuasion, including the application of hickory switches, the redman maintained his stubbornness. They assured him that his life would be spared, but he only bowed his head and said, "White man may tomahawk Indian, but Indian go no farther with white man."   They even threatened to kill him if he did not comply with their wishes, but he again bowed his head and refused.   This time his head did not resume its upright position, for a tomahawk descended and the redman was freed permanently from earthly cares.   The two Whites came home disappointed that they had only two scalps instead of a lively prisoner to show their friends.[45]

(6) Jacob Wetzel

Like his other brothers, Jacob Wetzel, great-great-grandfather of the present writer, had some brushes with the common enemy.   He and Simon Kenton[46] while on a fall hunt near the mouth of the Kentucky River, ran on to an abandoned Indian camp.   Neither a Kenton nor a Wetzel would think of backing out of such a vicinity without mak-

---

45.   True, according to Bonnett to Draper, *Draper's Mss.* 11E133 in the State Historical Society of Wisconsin, Madison, Wisconsin. This was in 1789, when they were spies.

46.   Simon Kenton was born in Virginia in 1755.   He went to Kentucky at the age of 17 and became a hunter, trapper and scout renowned for his skill and daring.   During the Revolution he became associated with Boone and fought with him at the battle of Painted Creek.   Later he was captured with three others while stealing horses from the Shawnee Indians in 1778.   This time Logan, chief of the Mingoes, saved his life.   Because of the name he had along the border as an Indian fighter he underwent terrible torture at their hands. They tied him to a wild horse and drove it through the forest.   He was made to run the gauntlet eight times and was thrice tied to the stake for execution.   At one instance he was saved by the intercession of Simon Girty the notorious renegade.   At another time he mystified the Indians with his burning glass, thus escaping what seemed to be certain death.   He was finally taken by the English and escaped from one of their military prisons.   He and the Wetzel brothers, especially Jacob, had many encounters with the Indians together.   He died in 1836.

ing his presence known, so the two determined to delay their hunt for deer until they had landed bigger game.

That night they heard guns fired; the next morning more guns, while in the distance could be seen a soft haze which told of an Indian camp. The hunters moved cautiously toward the smoke and that evening came in sight of the camp. Concealing themselves until dark they crept forward until they could see five men and five blankets.

"When shall it be?" whispered Jacob.

"Now, if you say so," responded Kenton. On second thought it was decided to await daylight, Kenton maintaining that "We had better have light and an open field."

They crouched down behind a large fallen tree and awaited the coming of day. When it was light enough to aim Jacob whispered, "I am glad I have a double-barreled rifle."

"Hush!" said Simon. "Now! And when my foot moves fire."

At the signal two rifles cracked and two redmen fell. Jacob fired his second barrel and dropped another camper. Yelling to scare the victims the white men rushed on the camp. Without ceremony the two remaining Indians fled in different directions.

Kenton chased one and soon returned with his scalp. Wetzel was not in camp, so Simon shouted for him. A faint answer came from afar. In a few minutes Jacob came bounding in with the scalp of the fifth Indian. "Now let us hurry," he said, "and begin our deer hunt."

"On October 7, 1790, Jacob Wetzel was at Fort Washington, where Cincinnati, Ohio, now stands, engaged in his usual occupation, hunting. The country was covered with a dense forest of beech and maple with an undergrowth of spice wood and grape vines, making a remarkably fine hiding place for lurking Indians as well as an excellent resort for deer.

"One day Jacob went out to hunt, as usual accompanied by his dog. The success of the day compelled him to return for a horse on which to carry his game, as it was too heavy a load for him to carry. While on the way he sat on a log to rest, his dog lying at his feet. While resting there he heard a rattle of leaves which caused the dog to growl. He silenced the dog, sprang behind a tree and looked in the direction of the dog's attention.

"An Indian a short distance from him, partly concealed by the trunk of a tree, was spied. The Indian had his gun in his hands ready for any emergency and appeared to be looking for danger, probably having heard the low growl of the dog. The dog now saw the Indian and barked aloud, giving notice of the presence of Wetzel. Both men raised their guns and fired at the same time at each other. The Indian's gun fell from his hands. The bullet from Wetzel's gun had struck his left arm and broken it at the elbow while Wetzel was uninjured by the bullet fired by the Indian.

"Jacob now rushed on the Indian with his knife. The red man warded off the thrust with such skill and force that he knocked the knife out of Wetzel's hand and threw it thirty feet from him. Wetzel attacked the Indian, although his adversary had his knife in his right hand. He caught him about the body, encircling his right arm, while the Indian still held his knife in his right hand. They engaged in a doubtful struggle, apparently with equal chances.

"The Indian struggled to get his right arm from the grasp of Wetzel, while the latter was endeavoring to prevent him. In their struggle their feet became interlocked and both fell to the ground, the Indian uppermost. This released his right arm from Wetzel's grasp. He was intending to use the knife while Wetzel was forcing him over on his right side to prevent him from using it. The Indian with a yell and all the exertion of his strength turned Wetzel under him and was about to plunge the knife into the white man when the dog, which so far had been silent, sprang upon the Indian, seizing him by the throat with such force that the red dropped the knife from his hand.

"Wetzel now threw the Indian from him, seized his knife and with his foot planted firmly upon the Indian's breast, he plunged it to the hilt into his heart. The savage gave one convulsive shudder, and was no more. As soon as Wetzel possessed himself of his rifle together with the Indian's weapons, he started on his way. He had gone but a short distance, when his ears were assailed by the startling whoops of a number of Indians. He ran eagerly for the river, but fortunately, finding a canoe on the beach near the water, was soon out of reach, and made his way without further danger to the cave at the foot of Sycamore street. The Indians came up to the place of the recent encounter and discovered the body of a fallen comrade. They gave a most hideous yell when, upon examination, they recognized in the dead Indian the features of one of their bravest chiefs."[47]

Extract from Letter of Lewis Bonnett to Lyman Draper, June 30, 1847

"You wish to know the year when Jacob Wetzel killed the two Indians by the help of his false man.

"The precise year I do not recollect; but to the best of my recollection, in the beginning of 1786 there was a kind of interim of peace and promised treaties of peace with all the neighboring tribes, but alas its progress was of but short duration, and marked by acts of general hostilities all around the Western settlements, and many acts of barbarity were committed. The autumn of that year and the ensuing year, 1787, was called the Bloody Year; and in the year 1787, in the spring, there was a fort building on my father's farm, and the neighbors would fort in the summer and retire to their farms in the winter, and continued so until the summer of 1787, -8, or perhaps -9.

"The Wetzel boys made a false face out of a soft

---

47.   From Henry Howe's *Historical Collections of Ohio*, Vol. II, 1888.

block of wood, and painted it a human color and fixed it in the human shape, and some of them would frequently go and see to the domestic concerns on their farms. Jacob taking his false man and his sister, Susannah by name (commonly called Susan) and staying all night, was apprehensive that there were Indians near, by the alarm of the dog in the night. He told his sister he had every reason to believe there were Indians near.

"As soon as it was fairly light, he opened the door, taking his post on the left side of the door, and Susannah on the right side. As the door opened to the right, she stood rather back of the door, holding up the false man with her left hand in full view of the open door. Two Indians were concealed some distance in front of the house. One of them fired at the false man, thinking it was the man of the house. The Indians rose from behind their concealment and made toward the house, but as soon as the report of the Indian's gun was heard, Susan let the false man fall in the house. Jacob shot one dead on his approach, and Susan quickly shut and bolted the door. Jacob soon had powder in his gun, and ramming two naked bullets down, fired out of a port hole just as the Indian was in the act of making off, the two balls taking effect in the Indian's back and soon brought him to the ground.

"You will remember that this same Susan was afterward married to a man named Nathaniel Goodrich, and her firstborn was a son named George, who married the only surviving daughter of the Tush family. The poor little infant was taken by the heels and struck against a stump in the yard when the rest of her family were murdered. Mary is still living, and has given birth to seven children, and resides with her husband on a good farm in the state of Indiana."[48]

48. Bonnett to Draper, *Draper's Mss.* 11E91 and 11E92 of the State Historical Society of Wisconsin, Madison, Wisconsin.

Jacob Wetzel

"Some years after Ohio County, Virginia, was organized and formed from West Augusta County, Virginia, in 1776, Jacob Wetzel was elected a magistrate, and then in turn, (as was the custom and law at that time, that the oldest magistrate should become sheriff of the county and collect the revenue) he became sheriff of Ohio County, Virginia, in 1803 and through dishonest deputies and other courses he became involved financially. It took all of his lands and property, and also all of his brother John's property, as he had that "brotherly love" for Jacob. After this, Jacob was both embarrassed and quite poor, and he resolved, in 1808, to emigrate to the West. He settled in Boone County, Kentucky, where he resided until 1811. Then he went still farther West and settled near Laurel, Franklin County, Indiana, and lived there until 1818, when he settled near the Bluffs, or Waverly, in Morgan County, Indiana, on the White River."[49-50-51-52]

On the Wetzel trace near where it crossed Flat Rock, an Indian named "Big Buffalo", was killed by his comrades in the summer of 1819. "Buffalo" had twelve months before

---

49. From John H. B. Nowland's *Early Reminiscences of Indianapolis*, 1820 to 1876. Published and Copyrighted 1877. Vol. I. Also John H. B. Nowland's *Prominent Citizens of Indianapolis*, 1876. Published and Copyrighted, 1877. Vol. II. Both published in Indianapolis, Ind.

50. George Wetzel, son of John, Jr., wrote Lyman C. Draper, that his uncle Jacob was wasteful and improvident and that his father's old farm went to pay Jacob's debts. *Draper's Mss.* 24S59 in the State Historical Society of Wisconsin, Madison, Wisconsin.

51. Cyrus Wetzel, son of Jacob, wrote Lyman C. Draper that when his father was sheriff of Ohio County, Va., his deputies defaulted and that his father gave up the homestead and all his personal property to satisfy the claim. *Draper's Mss.* 820S10 in the State Historical Society of Wisconson, Madison, Wisconsin.

52. *Order Book 9, page 142* in the Clerk of the County Courts office in the Courthouse at Wheeling, W. Va., gives the following: Jacob Wetzel came into court and gave bond as sheriff of Ohio County, Va., with Joseph Wilson as security for conditions for collecting the county levy for the year 1803. Joseph Caldwell or William Perrine as deputies. Jacob was later summoned into court and the distrust of the deputies was agreed to and the bond was paid in cash by Jacob Wetzel and John Wetzel, Jr., to relieve his security, Joseph Wilson of the payment.

killed an Indian called, "Old Solomon". The usual time of twelve moons was given him either to pay $100, one hundred buckskins, or forfeit his life. The band was encamped at this place when the time expired, and he was accordingly butchered and left lying in the middle of the Wetzel trace. He was buried by some Whites who found him.

In the fall of 1819, a party of Delaware Indians visited Jacob Wetzel, at his house. One of them was a very large and powerful brave named "Nosey", from the fact that he had lost part of his nose. This Indian proposed shooting at a mark with Jacob Wetzel's son, Cyrus. The young man beat him badly; but soon discovering that the Indian was very angry, and disposed to be quarrelsome about it; young Wetzel proposed to shoot again, and this time he let the Indian beat him as badly as he had previously beaten him before, which had the effect of pacifying him, at least for awhile. The Indians then left Wetzel's cabin and had gone about two miles when "Nosey" killed one of his comrades. It was supposed the anger engendered by being beaten by Wetzel's son had not yet cooled. "Nosey" was given the usual twelve moons to pay the price of life, which he had failed to do; and in the fall of 1820 "Nosey" was killed by the friends of the man he had murdered. At the expiration of the twelve moons he gave himself up. He was taken to a tree, his arms drawn up to a limb, his legs parted, his ankles fastened to a stake driven into the ground, and then he was stabbed under the arms and in the groins with a butcher knife, and tortured in other ways until his life was extinct.

In the spring of 1820 the body of a man was found about one and a half miles above the Bluffs. A man named Ladd was suspected of the murder. He was arrested by a set of desperate men who had banded together styling themselves as "Regulators". However, he was soon released, since there was not a shadow of evidence against him. He then sued for false imprisonment, and they were taken to Connersville for trial. This was the first case of litigation in the "New Purchase", and a very expensive one it proved to be. The case occupied a long time and finally resulted in the plaintiff getting nominal damages. This man was no doubt murdered by a desperate and notorious Delaware Indian named "Hiram Lewis"; for he was in possession of the murdered man's horse, saddle, bridle, pistol, and a red Morocco pocketbook containing some money on the Vincennes Steam Mill Company for which the murdered man was working at the time of his death.

Jacob Wetzel one day loaned a Delaware Indian his gig to spear fish and when it was returned, one of the prongs was gone, the Indian stating that he had broken it off in a log. A few days later, Mr. Wetzel came upon the same Indian on the river where he had speared a wagon load of the finest fish, with a gig made from the broken prong, which had been driven into the end of a tough, slender pole. The Indian was engaged in drying the fish. He was so expert that he could strike a fish eight or ten yards away. Many years ago the Wetzels discovered about a half bushel of bullets of all sizes, from a shot to a half ounce ball, on a bottom near Waverly. They had been scattered out over several rods of land, by the action of the water, no doubt, but how they came there is a mystery yet to be solved.

The following incident is told in the exact words of W. O. Baker, of Martinsville, Indiana. "Years ago when a boy I visited the home of Aunt Sally Goss, mother of Joe Hussey Goss, who lived near Paragon, and in that home were two long barreled rifles that were used by her husband, Ephriam Goss, in their pioneer days. At that time the names of Lewis Wetzel and Daniel Boone were household words, and one of the rifles was named 'Old Lewis', and the other was named 'Old Daniel', these names being bestowed on the rifles as a mark of esteem for these pioneer Indian fighters. I have fired both of these rifles"[53]

---

53. From Blanchard's *History of Morgan County, Indiana*, Vol. I, 1884.

Jacob Wetzel and Son Cyrus, the First Settlers of Morgan County, Indiana

Morgan County, Indiana, was a part of what is known in history as "The New Purchase", and was secured from the Indians by the treaty of St. Mary's, Ohio, entered into in October, 1818. The natives were to have the privilege of residing upon the soil and hunting thereon until 1820. The land could not be formally thrown upon the market until the expiration of this privilege of occupancy, but Whites could enter the territory, select their farms and improve the same and be ready to purchase when the land became marketable.

In the summer of 1818, before the lands of "The New Purchase", had been ceded to the government by the Indians, Jacob Wetzel went to the camp of the Delaware chief Anderson, whose principal village was where the city of Anderson now stands, to get permission to cut a trace from White Water river in the eastern part of the state to the Bluffs on White river, the object being to secure a road from such eastern point to the Bluffs, the remainder of the way to Vincennes to be the river.

Jacob Wetzel had in view then a permanent location at or near Vincennes. Permission was granted by Anderson, and the following autumn Jacob Wetzel, accompanied by his son Cyrus, and several hired men supplied with axes, guns, provisions, etc., blazed his route through to the Bluffs.

This blazed road was the first in this state and became a famous highway for families seeking homes in the New Purchase. It may yet be seen in some places and is still known as Wetzel's Trace.

Wetzel was so pleased with the Bluffs that he resolved to go no farther toward Vincennes, with a view of settlement, whereupon he selected a piece of land in the valley of the White river.

Up to this time no white men, save John and William Conner, who did business as traders with the tribe of Indians, dared to intrude upon their soil.

About March 15, 1819, Jacob Wetzel and his son Cyrus came on foot, via Wetzel's Trace to the Bluffs, with the necessary seeds, axes, guns and provisions. After selecting a tract of rich bottom land of about sixty acres just below Waverly, they proceeded to stake the permanent boundary and erected a rude log cabin. The father then went back to the family, leaving Cyrus, who was 19 years old, to clear immediately a few acres for a crop of corn, wheat, and vegetables and deaden a larger tract during the summer.

The second night after the father had gone a heavy snow fell and Cyrus built a large fire to drive off the wolves and the cold. During the night he felt something crawl under the blanket under which he was sleeping, but was too unconcerned to make further discoveries until the next morning, when he was somewhat surprised to learn that his sleeping companion was none other than a huge Delaware Indian. This discovery was not sufficient to scare perceptibly a man in whose veins ran the distinguished blood of the Wetzels. He felt no fear of the wilderness, though surrounded with wild and dangerous animals and scarcely less wild and dangerous Indians.

Cyrus Wetzel related this story to John H. B. Nowland and told him that he was glad to find he had a companion who would remain with him until his father returned; and one that furnished the camp with meat while he proceeded with his work in the clearing. He further stated that he felt as secure there alone with the untutored son of the forest as if he had been surrounded with Whites.

The following autumn when Jacob Wetzel removed his family to his new home he was soon followed by other families who would remain in camp over night near the Wetzel cabin to rest themselves and their jaded horses and oxen.[54]

----

54. From Blanchard's *History of Morgan County, Indiana,* Vol. I, 1884; and John H. B. Nowland's *Prominent Citizens of Indianapolis, Indiana.* Vol. II, 1876.

Jacob Wetzel's Death

"Captain Jacob Wetzel died on July 27, 1827. He took a very active part in all the Indian Wars in the West, including Pennsylvania, Virginia, and what is now the state of Ohio. He carried many testimonials of his bravery in the numerous wounds that he received in the various combats with the savage foe while in the army under Generals Harrison, St. Clair, and several other commanders. He performed very laborious duties and rendered signal service as a spy. He was most admirably adapted by his former life for these duties which he performed."[55]

John H. B. Nowland said, "I remember Jacob Wetzel as a square built, broad shouldered, muscular, and powerful man, five feet eleven inches in height, about 250 pounds in weight, without any surplus flesh, but of a fair proportion for such a frame. He died at the age of 62 years and is buried in what is known as the McKinsey cemetery, which is located on a hill just south of Waverly, Indiana, and along State road 37."[56]

(7) Cyrus Wetzel

"Cyrus Wetzel was born Dec. 1, 1800, in Ohio County, Virginia, at the old Wetzel homestead on Big Wheeling Creek.

"At the age of 19 he came to Waverly, Indiana, with his father, Jacob Wetzel, where he took up a claim and lived until his death. Before age began to tell on him he was as straight as an arrow; full six feet in height; hair as black as a raven; eyes equally as black, and as keen as a hawk. He was very prosperous, and accumulated a fortune for that day not by speculation of any kind but by in-

55. *Indianapolis Journal* of July 28, 1827.
56. Cyrus Wetzel's daughter married a McKinsey. The following gravestones are found in this cemetery: Jacob Wetzel, born Sept. 16, 1765, died July 27, 1827; Cyrus Wetzel, (son of Jacob) born Dec. 1, 1800, died Dec. 16, 1875; Elizabeth, wife of Cyrus Wetzel, born Nov. 10, 1803; died Oct. 17, 1864; Sabra Wetzel, wife of Charles Newton, born Feb. 22, 1798, died Jan. 20, 1822.

dustry and economy. In fact he literally dug it out of the earth. He owned one of the finest and best stocked farms in Indiana at the time of his death. He raised mostly beef cattle on the 500 acre farm. At his death he had fifty fine bullocks on his farm ready for the butcher's block. He was a man, of very general information, warm and devoted in friendship. He represented Morgan County, Indiana, in the legislature, where he was a very active and efficient member. He was an old line Whig, and when the party disbanded he went to the Republican party. During the Civil war he was a strong Union man. His son-in-law William McKinsey, was the only member of his family who was capable of bearing arms, and he enlisted the first year of the war and served three years.

"He was taken prisoner and served several months in Libby Prison at Richmond, Virginia.

"Cyrus Wetzel's home was a home for everyone. From his door no weary traveler was ever turned away hungry; no beggar empty-handed; no friend without an invitation to return again.

"The Wetzel farm has ·emained in the family to this day and his grandchildren are living on the same farm now, and it is known as the 'Wetzelwad' farm."[57]

Cyrus Wetzel's Letter to John H. B. Nowland

Waverly, Morgan County, Ind.,
March 10, 1870.

Mr. J. H. B. Nowland — Dear Sir;

Yours of the fourth inst. is received. The subject to which you call my attention I thought was settled many years since, i. e. John McCormack built the first house in Indianapolis in February, 1820. George Pogue settled on the bank of the creek, which takes its name from him, the following March. I am confident that there was not a white man living in Marion

57. From Blanchard's *History of Morgan County, Indiana.* Vol. I, 1884.

county in 1819. My father and self settled where I now live in the spring of 1819, when I was in my 19th year, and at an age calculated to retain any impression made on my mind.

Yours respectfully,

Cyrus Wetzel.

P. S.: Your statement in the Sentinel of the 25th ultimo is correct. My father and I came in the spring of 1819, say about the 15th of March, cleared ground raised a crop, and moved the family out in October following.

Cyrus Wetzel.

(8) Murder of the Tush Family

"The last murder by the Indians on Wheeling Creek, Virginia, was on Sept. 3, 1794, when a body of Indians and Peter Spicer, a white renegade, came to the house of George Tush and lay in ambush a short distance from the house until Tush went out to feed his hogs. Tush was resting his arms on the fence, and as the hogs came to the bars by the yard to receive their feed, the Indians fired at him. One ball struck him in the breast. He picked up his youngest child, who was in the yard, and ran into the house; the rest of the children, who were also in the yard, followed. He reached up to get his rifle from the hook and realized that his arm had been broken by the ball from the Indian's fire. He then ran out into the yard; one Indian was after him. George looked back over his shoulder and saw his wife for the last time. He ran with all speed to a high cliff of rocks which he jumped over and escaped to the cabin of Jacob Wetzel. The rest of the Indians entered the house, tomahawk in hand and began the horrid butchery of the rest of the family, seven in number. Beginning with the oldest daughter, Polly; then the next oldest, Nancy; then Susan; they thought that they had killed her, but she recovered. After the Indians had gone she came to, crawled into the house and was found lying on the hearth with her

head skinned down just about her ears. Mary, the infant.
the Indians took by the heels and knocked her against a
stump that stood in the yard. The poor little infant also
came to and crawled into the house, and lay with its head on
her sister Susan's breast. The rest they killed outright, and
scalped. They did not scalp little Mary, and she lived in
Indiana and raised a large family. She married George
Goodrich.

Fort Baker at the mouth of Grave Yard Run near Cresaps.
(Courtesy of The Wheeling-News Register)

"Susan survived until the third day of the following
March when she died, and my father, Lewis Bonnett, Sr.,
and myself dug her grave.

"The Indians took Mrs. Tush prisoner but in conse-
quence of her advanced state of pregnancy, she was not
able to travel rapidly. They took her about nine miles,
tomahawked and scalped her. She was not found for two
years, but her bones were collected and buried with the rest

of the family. Information was afterwards obtained from one that was a prisoner of the Indians at the same time, but who later escaped, that Mrs. Tush was tomahawked on a branch of Wheeling Creek, in a laurel thicket. It was shocking indeed when Martin and Jacob Wetzel, myself, and three other men accompanied George Tush back to his cabin the next day and found the mangled bodies of the ones that had been brutally murdered; and still worse mangled by the hogs."[58]

(9) The Battle of Captina

"One mile below the mouth of Captina, on the Virginia shore was Baker's fort, so-named for Captain John Baker. One morning in May, 1794, four men were sent over, according to the custom, to the Ohio side to reconnoiter.

"They were Adam Miller, John Daniels, Isaac McCowan and John Shoptaw. Miller and Daniels took upstream and the other two down. The upper scout was attacked and killed by Indians, and Miller killed. Daniels ran up to Captina, which was about three miles, but being weak from the loss of blood issuing from a wound in his right arm was taken prisoner and carried into captivity, but was subsequently released at the treaty of Greenville. The lower scouts having discovered signs of the enemy tried to effect their escape. Shoptaw swam across the Ohio river and escaped. McCowan was shot by the Indians while making up towards his canoe. He was wounded but had run down to the bank, and sprang into the water, pursued by the enemy, who overtook and scalped him. The firing was heard at the fort, and they asked for volunteers. There were fifty men in the fort. A daughter of Captain Baker volunteered to go saying she would be no coward. This aroused the pride of Captain Baker's son, John Baker, Jr., who before had determined not to go. He joined the others, fourteen in number, in command of Captain Enochs. They

58. Lewis Bonnett to Lyman C. Draper, *Draper's Mss.*, 11E87 in the State Historical Society of Wisconsin, Madison, Wisconsin.

soon crossed the river, and went up Captina single file, a distance of one and one-half miles, following the Indian trail. The enemy had come back on their own trail, and were in ambush on the hillside, awaiting their approach. When sufficiently near they fired upon the Whites but, being on an elevated position, the bullets passed harmlessly over them. The Whites then treed. Some of the Indians came behind and shot Captain Enochs and Mr. Hoffman. The Whites soon retreated, and the Indians pursued. When but a short distance John Baker was shot in the hip. Determined to sell his life as dearly as possible, he drew off on one side and secreted himself in a hollow with a rock at his back, offering no chance for the enemy but in front. Shortly after two guns were heard in quick succession. Doubtless one of them was fired by John Baker. From the signs afterwards it was supposed he had killed an Indian. The next day the men turned out and visited the spot. Enochs, Hoffman, and John Baker were found dead and scalped. Enochs' intestines and eyes were torn out, and Hoffman's eyes were screwed out with a wiping stick. The dead were wrapped in white hickory bark and brought over to the Virginia shore and buried in their bark coffins. There were about 30 Indians engaged in this action, and seven skeletons were found secreted in the crevices of rocks. Jacob, John, Jr., and Lewis Wetzel were along and took part in this fight. Governor McArthur was in this action also. He told McDonald in his biographical sketch that he was the youngest man of the fourteen that went out against the Indians and that after Captain Enochs was killed that he was called upon to direct the retreat. The wounded who were able to walk were placed in front, while McArthur and his Spartan band covered the retreat. The moment an Indian showed himself in pursuit he was fired upon and generally, it is believed, with effect. The Indians were so severely handled that they gave up the pursuit. The great Shawnee chief, Charles Wilkey, was in command of the Indians. He told the author McDonald that the battle of

Captina was the most severe conflict he ever witnessed, and that, although he had the advantage of ground and the first fire, he lost most of his men, half of them having been either killed or wounded. The three Wetzel brothers, Henry Baker, Reuben Roberts, George Baker, Leonard Reigor and two brothers, Aaron Hughes, Captain Roberts and three canoe loads from Round Bottom attended Captain Baker's funeral."[59-60]

(10) Lewis Bonnett and Lyman C. Draper's Letters

Union City, Ohio, Nov. 3, 1846.

My dear highly esteemed friend, Mr. Lyman C. Draper; The delay in answering your inquiries of last January has been due to illness. I have just written a letter to Asa Zane, son of Johnathan Zane, who lives in

---

59.   This narrative was told by Martin Baker, a brother of John Baker, who was 12 years old and an inmate of Baker's Fort at the time of the Battle of Captina. From Henry Howe's *"Historical Collections of Ohio,"* Vol. II, 1888. Colonel S. P. Baker stated that the three Wetzel's recovered Captain John Baker's body shortly after he was shot. He had crawled partly under a log, lying insensible, and was put on a canoe, carried across the river to the fort, where he soon died. His eyes were both gored out. He was buried near the fort or blockhouse at Grave Yard Run, near Cresap's.

60.   From the *Wheeling Intelligencer,* May 1866, Colonel Samuel P. Baker, from whom these facts were received, lived near Benwood, W. Va. He is the second son of Henry Baker, and was born in 1798. He married Caroline Tomlinson, the oldest daughter of Samuel Tomlinson, in 1825.

The following is from Samuel P. Baker:

"John Baker, my grandfather, was a Prussian. He came to the United States in 1755. He landed at Philadelphia, where he married a German lady named Elizabeth Sullivan, in 1760. After his marriage he moved to the Shenandoah valley of Virginia where, in 1773, Henry Baker, my father, was born. In 1767 he emigrated to Dunkard creek, Greene county, Pennsylvania, and settled among the Indians, four tribes of whom were living there in peace with the Whites, viz.; the Delawares, the Wyandottes, the Shawnees, and the Mingoes. He remained there until the breaking out of the Dunmore's war, when he took refuge with his family in what was then called Redstone Old Fort, now Brownsville, Pennsylvania. After Dunmore's war he settled at Cresap's Bottom, and built a fort or blockhouse that was commonly known as Baker's Station, and was a noted place for protection against the Indians. He was killed by the Indians on the Ohio side in 1778 in company with the three Wetzels and buried on the Virginia side near the blockhouse or fort."

Indiana, for the papers Mr. Zane alluded to in your letter.

I went to see old Captain Samuel Davis and his old lady, but the old lady departed this life last fall. I found the old man's mind very much impaired so that I could not get much satisfaction from him.

A few days after I returned home from visiting Davis I was taken ill of fever which continued on until two weeks ago. Mr. Curry presented your letter to me a few days ago, which contained the inquiries as my letter from you. I am now able to write and will answer for both.

Regarding the adventure of Lewis Wetzel, in 1787 or 1788, I will give it to you as he told me with his own mouth.

He made his home with my father on Wheeling Creek at that time. He started crossing the Ohio river and penetrating the Indian country. He discovered an Indian camp near the west bank of the Ohio river. The fire was still burning and Wetzel concealed himself nearby waiting with patience the return of an Indian. At last there were three that made their appearance. One was an old Indian carrying his rifle and a deer skin. The other two were young lads, probably his sons, carrying their bows and arrows. Lewis waited with anxiety until they got safely around their fire. The old Indian put his gun in the back of the camp. Lewis concluded that the proper time had come, and he took deliberate aim at the old Indian with his old "kill devil". As soon as he pulled the trigger he rushed on the young Indians calling aloud to come on, signifying that there were more with him. The young Indians took to flight. Lewis pursued and soon had his gun reloaded. He could easily outrun the young braves and coming up close to them he shot one through the body. The young Indian sank to the ground the blood coming from his mouth. Lewis soon dispatched him with his

tomahawk, and made his way back to the camp, scalped
the one there and made his way for home. Upon his
return he was asked what luck he had, his reply was,
"Poor". I treed three but got only two of them, at the
same time pulling the two scalps from his shot pouch.

Your esteemed friend,
Lewis Bonnett.[61]

Philadelphia, Pa.,
Nov. 1, 1848.

My dear friend Bonnett;

The summer past I changed my residence from
Baltimore to this city.

Just before coming here I visited Washington City,
and had a fine visit with William Dailey. We went to
call on Mrs. Cruger (formerly Lydia Boggs) and it
was a pleasant one, I assure you.

I wish to obtain information from you about the
following:

First: Some one, two or three years before Dunmore's War in 1774, there was an Indian named Bald
Eagle killed while descending the Monongahela river
in a canoe. Do you know anything of the history of
this incident?

Second: About that time a party of Whites destroyed Bulltown on the Little Kanawha, and killed
several Indians. Do you know anything of this?

Third: There was an Indian named Jacob killed
before Dunmore's War on Dunkard's Creek. Do you
know anything about the particulars of this affair?

Fourth: A white man named Crago was killed by
the Indians west of the Monongahela river in what is
now Greene County, Pennsylvania, sometime before
Dunmore's War. Do you know how it happened?

Fifth: Do you know of any other William Shep-

---

61. Bonnett to Draper, *Draper's Mss.*, 11E83 and 11E84, of the
State Historical Society of Wisconsin, Madison, Wisconsin.

herd, besides Colonel David Shepherd's son of that name, who was killed at the first siege of Wheeling? Did he ever live on Dunkard or Whiteley?

Sixth: Have you any recollections of hearing that one of the McMahons or McMechen's had horses stolen from below Wheeling by the Indians just before Dunmore's War? What were the facts?

Seventh: How long was John Grist kept a prisoner, how did he escape, and when did he return to Wheeling? What became of him?

Eighth: Was there a Captain Abraham Keller on Wheeling Creek? If so, what was his history, and what became of him?

If any new incidents about your cousins, the Wetzels, occur to you, will you please state them to me?

Your obliging friend,

Major Lewis Bonnett   Lyman C. Draper.[62]
Near Maysville, Ohio.

Union City, Ohio., Dec. 18, 1848.

My dear Friend Draper;

I shall try to answer your inquiries of Nov. 1, 1848. My father told me that Bald Eagle was killed in 1767. Fort Bedstone, now Brownsville, Pa., was settled by a few families who were: Abraham Tegard; James Crawford, the brother of the unfortunate Colonel Crawford who was burned at the stake at Sandusky, Ohio; John Province and John Harden. In the same year, 1767, Thomas Decker, David Morgan and others settled near where Morgantown now stands. In 1769, Colonel Ebenezer Zane, Silas Zane and others settled at Wheeling.

In the fall of 1764, or it may have been 1767, my father, Lewis Bonnett, with his company and John

---

62. *Bonnett's Mss.* from Draper 11E109 to 11E113 inclusive, of the State Historical Society of Wisconsin, Madison, Wisconsin.

Wetzel's family, his brother-in-law, settled on Big Wheeling Creek from the forks up. I think that David Shepherd came in 1769 or 1770. Jacob Van Metre, John Swan, Thomas Hughes and others settled on the west side of the Monongahela where Carmichael, Pa., now stands on Muddy Creek, Greene County, Pennyslvania.

In 1772 emigrants began to flow rapidly into that beautiful country called the Upper Monongahela and the Ohio Valley.

Robert Cunningham, Henry Fink, John Goff, John Miner, Robert Butler, William Morgan and others settled on Dunkard's Bottom. The unfortunate Thomas Eckerly settled on the Horseshoe Bottom nearby Captain Thomas Parsons.

The same year settlements were made on Simpson's Creek and on Elk River. My father sold his property on Big Wheeling Creek and moved to the Monongahela and settled near the mouth of Dunkard Creek. When old Bald Eagle was murdered he was friendly to the Whites. He was found alone by Jacob Scott, William Hacker, and Elijah Runner who murdered him in the following way: They tied and seated him in the stern of a canoe, stuffed a piece of "Johnny cake" in his mouth and set him adrift on the Monongahela River. His body was found floating near the shore about the mouth of George's Creek, where Geneve now stands. Mrs. Province, the wife of John Province, discovered the body, had it brought ashore and decently buried, which was the end of old friend Bald Eagle. I do not know to what tribe he belonged.

A settler named Ryan is blamed for the killing of the Indian named Jacob, but I call the Indian Peter. Ryan declared that he would kill every Indian he met.

A white man named Crago was killed by the Indians in 1773, or 1774, in Greene County, Pennsylvania.

There were eight Indians in this party led by the celebrated Chief Logan.

Two or three Indians were killed on the South branch by Henry Judah and Nicholas Harpath while paying the Whites a friendly visit. Judah was arrested and confined in prison, but he was soon released when 200 men went to the prison and protested against it. The Indians at Bulltown were accused of murdering the Stroud family in 1772, on the Gauley River and stealing all their horses and cattle.

A party of Whites under William White and a man named Dorman marched on the Indians at Bulltown and slaughtered them all and stole their horses and cattle. This was in 1774.

I never knew any other William Shepherd except Colonel David Shepherd's son, but there was a family named Shepherd that settled on Grave Creek near Moundsville, and he told me that his grandfather was killed in the first siege of Fort Henry at Wheeling.

A man named James McMahon, also called Jimsy McMahan, lived on Dunkard Creek. He sold his possessions there, went to Pittsburgh and joined Lord Dunmore's army in 1774. He settled near Wheeling shortly after Dunmore's campaign. He later settled near the mouth of Fish Creek, on the Ohio River.

John Grist was kept a prisoner by the Indians for six years. He hunted with them and was granted certain privileges. He was taken to Detroit and set free, and came to Wheeling in 1788. He married Rachel Howell, who later died and he then married again and moved to the state of Ohio. His daughter Rachel was tomahawked and scalped by the Indians but survived and married Henry Jolly; but in later years her wound caused her death as the wound never healed over the bone of her head. She bore Henry Jolly several children. After his wife's death Henry Jolly married an old woman to care for his children. He died at Marietta, Ohio.

There never was a Captain Abraham Keller on Wheeling Creek, but a Martin Keller settled three miles above my father on Wheeling Creek. My father was the only Captain on Wheeling Creek at this time, and was succeeded as Captain by Henry Jolly.

Your obliging friend,

Lewis Bonnett.[63]

Philadelphia, Pa.,

Dec. 22, 1848.

My dear Friend;

On the first of November last I wrote you about a few inquiries and have not had the pleasure to hear from you in reply. The next day after writing you I went to Albany and Boston, and was absent four weeks. I secured a fine addition to my store of historical collections.

Still delayed and disappointed in getting some additional facts and documents for my Clark works, I concluded, while waiting to get them altogether complete, I would set about to prepare my intended work on the pioneers of the Upper Ohio, the Wetzels, Captain Brady, your father, Colonel Shepherd, the McColloch's, and Colonel Crawford. So I have been very busy in looking over all the dates and notes together with all I have about the Wetzels, from you and others, and weighing and comparing them. I hope that you, an old pioneer and old soldier will not get alarmed at the long list of my inquiries, and its formidable character; but set yourself down and reply as well as you can, if your health will permit and I hope and pray that it may. The fuller you write them out the better. I hope

---

63.   Bonnett to Draper, *Draper's Mss.*, 11E114 to 11E119 inclusive, of the State Historical Society of Wisconsin, Madison, Wisconsin. James McMahon was born Aug. 25, 1748, and died Aug. 3, 1824. He served as a private in the 2 Bn. Wash. Co. Militia, Rev. War. He is buried near Kent, Marshall County, W. Va.

in a few months that I will be able to send you a
printed volume of the services of your ancestors and
kinsmen in which your own work will figure promi-
nently and patriotically for your devoted kindness and
faithfulness which will be thankfully acknowledged.

It has been about four weeks since I heard indirect-
ly that our good friend William Dailey was unusually
well. I remain

Most sincerely, your obliging friend,

Major Lewis Bonnett   Lyman C. Draper.[64]
Maysville,
   Union County,
      Ohio.

' Philadelphia, Pa.,
Dec. 22, 1848.

My dear friend Major Lewis Bonnett;

Will you please answer the following inquiries to
the best of your knowledge?

When Captain John Wetzel lived on the South
Branch did he take any part in the old French and
Indian War? What was his age, size, appearance, and
character? Was it not on the South side of Wheeling
Creek that Captain Wetzel lived?

Was your father or any of the Wetzels out in Mc-
Intosh's campaign in the fall of 1778?

Was Lewis Wetzel present at the treaty at Fort
McIntosh in 1785? If so, did he meet some of his old
Indian friends and go to their towns with them to
visit?

Was George Edgington in the Beaver Blockhouse
affair with Captain Samuel Brady, in the spring of
1791?

Can you tell me about Jacob Wetzel, Alexander Mitchell and Peter Crow killing an Indian?

64. Lyman C. Draper to Lewis Bonnett, *Bonnett's Mss.*, 11E20
to 11E26 inclusive, of the State Historical Society of Wisconsin,
Madison, Wisconsin. Draper died before his works were published.

Did Captain Samuel Brady make an extraordinary leap across some stream to escape from the Indians?

Do you know anything of Isaac Meeks, William McIntire, James Lemon, Henry Hoagland, and Conrad Stoup?

Can you tell me of Major Rose's death?

Do you know anything of John Wetzel, Jr.'s death?

Your obliging servant,

Lyman C. Draper.[65]

Union City, Ohio, Jan. 24, 1849.

My dear friend Draper;

I shall try to answer your inquiries as follows: Captain John Wetzel did not take any part in the old French and Indian War. He was of ordinary size, stout and muscular, black piercing eyes, and black hair. The farm was situated in a large bend in the creek, and on the north side of the creek.

No, neither my father, Lewis Bonnett, Sr., nor any of the Wetzels were out in McIntosh's campaign.

The McIntosh treaty is correct. Do you think that Lewis Wetzel would make a friendly visit to an Indian town? I would say he would not. Lewis Wetzel kept his word of peace with the Hurons but he never abandoned his quests after the Delaware tribes it is said.

The Beaver Blockhouse affair is as near correct as I can make it. Jacob Wetzel, Alexander Mitchell, and Peter Crow went into the Indian country with the intentions of taking an Indian companion. They found a camp of three Indians. They hid and watched their maneuvers. In the evening two went off and left one to keep camp. Wetzel and his comrades slipped up in the night and killed him instead of taking him alive. This was in 1792.

It is true about Captain Samuel Brady leaping over

65. Draper to Bonnett, *Bonnett's Mss.*, 11E20 to 11E26 inclusive of the State Historical Society of Wisconsin, Madison, Wisconsin.

a deep ravine. Isaac Meeks lived on Grave Creek. He later moved to Knox County, Ohio, and then to Belmont County, Ohio, where he died. His widow moved back to Knox County, where his daughter married a Barkus.

William and Conrad McIntire both died on Wheeling Creek. The McIntires are still living in that country, some in Kentucky, and some in Ohio.

Major Ezekiel Rose lived in Greene County, Pa. One of his sons married a granddaughter of Captain John Wetzel.

Your obliging servant, Lewis Bonnett.[66]

(11) Peter Spicer

This story is as Lewis Bonnett related it to Lyman C. Draper.

"The Spicer family was destroyed in 1777. My mother related the following story to me about the Spicer family:

"When the people broke up in the Wheeling country and on Wheeling Creek, all the families packed up and were conducted on by Captain John Wetzel. My father, Lewis Bonnett, stayed behind in order to waylay the trail, until the families were out of danger. When Uncle John Wetzel and the families reached a place called Meadow Run, thinking that they were safe; they made a halt to rest for a day or two.

"Uncle John C. Sickes (or Sykes,) then living near the mouth of Dunkard Creek, upon hearing of the arrival of the Wheeling families at Meadow Run, saddled his horse and rode to meet them to inquire of the danger. He soon returned and said to my mother, 'Elizabeth, pack up quick,

---

66. George Wetzel told Draper in 1845 that his father John Wetzel, Jr., was ill only two days and died at his home on Wheeling Creek, in May, 1817, aged 47 years. He was buried in a cemetery on a hill about two miles southeast of the homestead, known as the McCreary cemetery. Bonnett to Draper, *Draper's Mss..* 11E27 to 11E37 inclusive, and George Wetzel to Draper, *Draper's Mss.,* 2S311 and 23S60, of the State Historical Society of Wisconsin, Madison, Wisconsin.

I am going to take you away for in my opinion you are not safe here'. They were soon on their way with the other movers, and after traveling about one and a half or two miles they passed Spicers' house. The inmates came out and inquired what news. The answer was, bad enough, that the Indians would murder all the settlers on the Ohio unless they vacated. The movers were not out of hearing of the guns, when the Indians appeared at Spicer's house. Hearing the guns and noise the movers made all speed and all escaped. That same day my father followed the movers' trail and found that the Indians had fallen in on their trail. He was much alarmed when he came to Meadow Run and found no one there. He proceeded on to Spicers' and found that the family had just been murdered; hurrying on the Indians' trail he was pleased to find that the Indians did not follow the movers' trail any farther. My father, of course, followed the movers' trail and found them all safe with his brother-in-law, John C. Sickes (or Sykes.)

"Peter Spicer and several of his brothers and sisters were captured by the Indians and taken prisoner, when the rest of the family was murdered. Peter lived with the Indians so many years that he finally turned against the Whites and joined the Indians in their depredations, such as the Tush massacre in 1794. Other prisoners returning from the Indian towns as captives all agree that Peter Spicer was a cruel tyrant to other prisoners. He was also very active in going with Indian parties against the Whites, and was often seen riding a fine horse that he had stolen from the White settlements, as well as prisoners and scalps. Some years after Wayne's treaty, Peter Spicer tried to gain possession of his father's plantation, that he owned when Peter was captured, and his father killed, but he was not successful in securing it. Peter Spicer lived and died on the Sandusky in 1815."[67]

67. Lewis Bonnett to Lyman C. Draper. *Draper's Mss.*, 11E35 and 11E36 in the State Historical Society of Wisconsin, Madison, Wisconsin.

(12) Lewis Himself

One day in the fall of 1789 while Lewis and Jacob Wetzel were hunting near where Majorsville, Marshall County, now stands on the waters of Wheeling Creek they spied seven Indians sitting on a log. The Indians not knowing the Whites were near were in the most gleeful mood. The Wetzel brothers crept forward like mice. Jacob crept to a rear position while Lewis established himself on the flank. At a given signal both fired. Jacob killed one redskin and Lewis two, his bullet going through the nearest and into the next. The other four ran in different directions, the Whites pursued and after a long chase succeeded in getting another scalp each. Two of the Indians escaped.

On May 25, 1782, the ill-fated Crawford punitive expedition started.[68] Lewis Wetzel joined the campaign against his mother's wishes.

"He never minded me," she said, "and he don't care if we all are murdered, so that he can go murder himself. It is his place to stay here and protect us, instead of doing as he does."

Bertha Rosencranz did not approve of his activities either. At one time he was preparing for an Indian hunt when he found her crying.

"What ails you, Bertha?" he inquired.

"Oh, Lewis Wetzel, why do you want to kill Indians? Stay here with us."

"If we all stayed here what would happen to us all?" Wetzel replied.

"You are so young, and I am afraid you will get killed. Let some of the older and more experienced men go hunt the Indians."

"I promised that I would go, and I must keep my promise," said Lewis.

---

68. Colonel William Crawford was born in Virginia. His son told Lewis Bonnett that Colonel Crawford and Colonel Stephans moved from Virginia to Washington County, Pa. *Draper's Mss.*, 11E86 in the State Historical Society of Wisconsin, Madison, Wisconsin.

To further entreaties on her part he responded with: "No, Bertha, you cannot detain me any longer than any other woman. Good-bye." He left the girl sobbing with her head against a tree.

It is rather strange that this arch enemy of the red man should show a consistent disregard for the pleadings of white women, but on at least two occasions he displayed solicitude for feminine members of the red race.

We are not told how Lewis escaped from the disastrous Crawford expedition, but following it we find him on the road between Wheeling and Washington, Pa., where he met a man named Mills[69] who had left his horse at a spring near Claysville. Mills asked Wetzel to help him get the horse. Wetzel warned the owner that the horse might be used as bait for a trap, and that Indians would get the man who tried to get the nag. But Mills thought he could take care of himself. Accordingly they proceeded toward the spring.

On the way to the spring they ran onto an Indian and a squaw sleeping by a little fire. The red man awoke to find Lewis' gun pointed at him. The Indian girl with a shriek threw herself before the brave. Her man then explained how they had run away from their tribe because of opposition to their marriage. Lewis lowered his gun, took the warrior's arm and said, "Go. The woman has made me break my vow. Go before I repent."

"Repent of what?"

"Of not killing you when I had the chance," said Wetzel.

"White man talk big," sneered the brave.

"Go," commanded Wetzel.

"It is the redman's land," said the Indian.

"Get him away," said Lewis to the girl.

She ran to her brave, begging him to leave. Lewis turned his back on the pair, and a bullet whistled close to

---

69. This was John Mills who was a brother of Thomas Mills that was killed at St. Clairsville, Ohio, by Indians two years before Lewis Wetzel was in this Indian fight at St. Clairsville when Thomas Mills was killed. Bonnett to Draper, *Draper's Mss.*, 11E29 in the State Historical Society of Wisconsin, Madison, Wisconsin.

his ear. The Indian had fired at the man who spared his
life. Turning on his heel Wetzel shot him and left the girl
wailing over his body.

This little chore out of the way, the two went on to get
the horse, which they discovered tied to a tree.

"Beware," said Lewis. "Treachery."

Mills walked up to the tree. A gun barked, and he fell
dead. Lewis took to his heels at top speed with a score of
redmen after him.

Wetzel's gun was always loaded. Lewis Wetzel's encounter
with the four Indians.

Down the leaf-strewn path he raced at breakneck speed.
He was one of the fleetest men of his time, and soon dis-
tanced his pursuers. After running about a mile he looked
back and saw that only four Indians were still following
him. He whirled and shot the foremost, leaving only three.
Again bringing into play his trick of loading as he ran he
turned to stop another red only to find that the pursuer
was upon him. The redman grasped the gunbarrel and as

Lewis later said, "He and the Indian had a severe wring."
But he wrenched the gun from the redskin's hands and put
an end to him with it.

The two remaining braves came on with caution. Every
time Lewis would turn to shoot they would dodge behind
trees. Eventually he caught them in a clearing and shot
the third. Upon this the fourth ran off exclaiming, "*Wooh!
wooh! No catch dat man. Him gun always loaded.*"[70]

When Lewis reached the settlement with his story and
the three scalps Bertha said, "Lewis Wetzel, you are a brave
man."

"I hope I am something," said Lewis modestly .

"Lewis, Charley Madison wants to marry me. Will you
advise me?"

"Yes. Marry him," said Wetzel, taking her hand.

She burst into tears. "Oh, how can you!" she sobbed.

"Bertha, I am sorry we do not understand each other."

"We do," she said.

"I don't know what you mean," said Wetzel.

"Explain," said Bertha.

"I always wondered why some real nice fellow hadn't
come along and married you," replied Lewis.

She looked at him thunderstruck, then bursting into
tears again struck at him.

"I do not understand, Bertha," he said.

---

70. W. Scott Powell's "*History of Marshall County.*" Thomas
Mills' cousin Joshua Davis, age 15, was in the fight at St. Clairsville,
Ohio. Mills was on his way home from the Crawford expedition in
1782. A few days later when they went back to bury Thomas Mills
at St. Clairsville, Ohio, they found that the bullet had broken his
ankle and the Indians had tomahawked him.

CHAPTER VI

THE FUGITIVE OF JUSTICE

TIMES must have been dull for a year or two; likely there was a depression in the scalp business. At any rate we do not hear of any escapades until 1785, when Lewis disappeared. It wasn't much loss. He was a morose sort, not good company, and when his trusty rifle was not needed to slay attacking reds the folks soon forgot him. At first there was the usual idle speculation.

"The Indians are not thick enough here for him," said the men.

"Bertha Rosencranz wants to be too thick with him," thought the women.

"He is too thick headed," was Bertha's opinion.

But Lewis was restless and content only when wandering around searching for adventures. What happened during the summer is unknown, as he was heard of only occasionally by hunters having seen him in the forest. He doubtless wandered far and kept up his unrelenting private war with the red race. In the fall he turned up at the settlement loaded down with scalps. No boastful stories of the summer's work were forthcoming. Lewis was never boastful, nor was he cruel; that is he never tortured victims as was the playful custom in those times.

He preferred the company of dogs and children to grown folks, and perhaps did not show such poor judgment in his choice. Seeing a man beating a dog Lewis promptly gave him the same treatment. Bertha Rosencranz, who must have kept pretty close tab on him, was there to see it and to exclaim: "Such a man!" dodging behind a tree that he might not see her.

After his summer's vacation communing with nature and collecting scalps he thought it fitting to tackle a serious job, so he went down the Ohio River with Major Doughty's expedition to build Fort Harmar where the Muskingum empties into the Ohio, now Marietta, Ohio.

General Harmar, who was in command of the fort, was trying to put over a peace treaty with the Indians and end the long unpleasant Indian war. Knowing Wetzel's habit of popping off an Indian and thinking afterward, if at all, the General looked with suspicion on this famous Indian fighter. His joking way of shooting a peace-making red-skin in the back might not promote the interests of permanent peace if allowed to function. So the General ordered Wetzel brought before him for instructions.

A settler remarked, "He must first be caught."

"He shall be," exclaimed the soldier. "I do not intend to have my project for peace set aside by one murderous man."

"Murderous. That's a hard word, General," replied the settler. "Lewis Wetzel never committed murder."

"What do you call murder?" asked the General.

"Killing Indians is not murder," replied the other. "Peace or no peace, Lewis Wetzel had better be left alone."

"Why?"

"You will find out." And he did, as later events will reveal.

Wherever Wetzel went a group of settlers would be tagging him around. The General soon discovered that they were there to defend the scout from the military authorities, In spite of the warning, or possibly because of it, Wetzel soon proved that the General's suspicions were well grounded, that this wild ranger of the woods was neither a diplomat nor a promoter of peace with the reds.

A large Indian was riding boldly toward the fort to talk peace with the General. Lewis and Veach Dickerson, hidden by the path, fired at the brave. He jumped as if stung by a yellow-jacket, but his horse dashed on and carried him into camp, dead. He had been shot through the hips and died from loss of blood while riding.

This was enough for the General, in fact too much. Furiously he exclaimed, "The murderer shall be caught and an example made of him. This is how my efforts for peace are regarded!" Thus we find Wetzel for the first time a fugitive from justice, but it is doubtful if he worried much about it.

Captain Kingsbury and a group of picked men were ordered to go to Mingo Bottom and take Wetzel, dead or alive. Old accounts say, "A company of men could have as easily drawn Beelzebub out of the bottomless pit as to take Lewis Wetzel from the Mingo Bottom settlement."

A shooting match was in progress when Kingsbury's company was seen approaching Mingo Bottom. Quickly a plot was formed to destroy the entire company by surprise, but Major McMahon, who was with the Mingo Bottom settlers, prevented this by persuading the hotheads to let him talk the matter over with Kingsbury. He told Kingsbury of the plot, also that the settlers approved of Wetzel and Dickerson killing the Indian and that further effort to seize Wetzel would bring the entire country upon the soldiers. This was so convincing that after consulting with his men five minutes Kingsbury commenced a retreat.

Dickerson stepped forward and said that since he shot at the Indian too, possibly he did the killing, but General Harmar wanted only Wetzel. His rebuff at Mingo Bottom did not end the affair. The General was beaten for the present, but he did not forget.

After the Kingsbury affair had blown over a little Wetzel and a friend named Hamilton Carr planned a trip to Kentucky. Carr lived on an island near Fort Harmar and the two stopped here for the night and to pay the folks a visit.

General Harmar learned that Wetzel was on the island, so about midnight sent a fleet of canoes from the fort to the island. The force of men they carried landed on the point of land farthest away from the cabin and sneaked quietly toward the abode.

Kingsbury knocked and demanded admission in the name of law and order. Carr opened the door, with a lantern in one hand and a rifle in the other. He was disarmed and held by the soldiers, while Wetzel was made prisoner before he could get out of bed. Considered something of

Kingsbury and his soldiers at the Carr Cabin demanding admission to capture Lewis Wetzel.

a desperado he was bound hand and foot, taken to the fort and there manacled with iron fetters and put into prison.

Restraint was about the hardest thing for young Wetzel to endure; and to be awaiting trial for killing an Indian seemed to him the height of injustice. He said he would never hang. "Imprisoned, broken-hearted, to all outward appearances crushed he yet maintains his lofty pride, and from his lowly prison cell looks down with scorn upon his brutal keepers," say the historians.

"Let me not live longer strangled and suffocated by their choking prison walls," he thought. It was in this state of mind that he made a proposition to General Harmar. "I have lived like a man," said the scout. "Let me die like one. Let the Indians form a circle. Place me in the center with no weapon but my knife, and let us fight until I am gone."

The General was so impressed by Wetzel's courage and fierce love of freedom that he ordered the fetters removed from his feet. He could then walk around and was taken out in the open for exercise under guard.

Rejoicing in his limited freedom he ran back and forth under the watchful eyes of the guards. When he went too far and they started after him he came trotting back and laughed at them. In this manner he ran a little farther each time until the guards refused to be teased into pursuing, then finding the guards off guard he made a dash and disappeared in the forest, still hand cuffed.

Whites and Indians searched four days for the escaped prisoner. At one time his pursuers sat down on a hollow log in which he was hiding, so close to him that he feared they would hear his heart beating. One of the Indians remarked, "No white man yet," adding what they would do with him when they caught him. But they did not catch him.

That night Wetzel crawled from his hiding place and got to the Ohio River. With his hands fettered swimming the river was no easy feat, but he made it. On the opposite shore he encountered Isaac Wiseman fishing. Wiseman got a file from a nearby blacksmith and removed the handcuffs.

From here Wetzel went to Charley Madison's cabin, where he spent the night. In the morning he borrowed a blanket and rifle and was ready for action again[71] Madison said, "Lewis, you haven't asked me why I have built this new cabin."

"I suppose it's because you wanted to," said the direct and simple-minded Lewis.

"Well, I'll tell you, Lewis. I'm going to be married."

"I wish you much happiness," said Lewis.

"But you haven't asked me who she is," said Madison.

"I'm not very inquisitive," said Lewis.

"Then I'll tell you. It's Bertha Rosencranz. I did think she cared for somebody else, but last week she told me that all men were cowards but me; she never saw such a world for cowards. She even said you were the biggest coward of all."

"All the same I wish you and her happiness. Good-bye," said Wetzel, as he started on his interrupted Kentucky hunt. He got as far down the river as Point Pleasant, W. Va., where he went ashore and spent several days among friends. Although he was still a fugitive from the military authorities he made no effort to conceal himself, and one day he unexpectedly met Captain Kingsbury on the street. Both men stopped, Wetzel planting himself in a defiant attitude but making no effort at violence. Kingsbury eyed him for a moment, then said, "Wetzel, get out of my sight." Wetzel passed on, ready for but not inviting trouble. Kingsbury made no effort to seize him.

Reaching Kentucky he was free again, for the time being. He made his headquarters at Washington, now Mason County, Ky., and spent his time roaming the forests. We have no record of the game he sought or took, but evidently for him the time was a welcome opportunity to enjoy the only kind of freedom he knew or cared for, that of the unfenced forest.

---

71.   This rifle that Lewis Wetzel borrowed from Charley Madison is now in the state museum at Charleston, West Virginia, with 23 notches on the stock for the 23 Indians that it is said he killed with it in a running fight.   He used it until 1794.

General Harmar moved his headquarters to Fort Washington, Cincinnati, Ohio, and one of his first official acts was to offer a reward "for the body of one Lewis Wetzel, an Indian scout well known to the frontier." Wetzel thought he was free, but he had the General still to cope with.[72]

If Lewis' pride was hurt at Bertha's choice he showed no signs of it. That is probably because he felt no regret, but might be because he encountered a potent remedy for broken hearts about this time.

---

72.   From Cecil B. Hartley's *"Life of Lewis Wetzel."*

CHAPTER VII

Lewis' Friendship and Early Associations
With Lydia

THE sunlight flashed from the regular dipping of a canoe paddle as a white girl propelled the fragile craft toward the wooded banks of the west side of the Ohio River. She landed on a likely stretch of sand and stepped out. A plumed warrior rushed from the shelter of overhanging trees and menaced her with uplifted tomahawk. Falling on her knees the girl begged for mercy. The savage burst into a laugh and exclaimed, "Why, don't you know me, Lydia?" It was Lewis Wetzel returning in Indian guise from a scouting trip.

The girl was Lydia Boggs, a child of the frontier who had learned to roam the woods, climb trees, swim the Ohio and shoot a rifle. She had been to Philadelphia attending a young ladies' school, where she learned other things not taught in the settlements. Beautiful and aristocratic this girl of spirit and culture must have seemed a creature from another world to the rough woodsman. And in his reckless daring the school girl saw much to be admired.

Lewis took supper with the young lady and later the two took a long stroll along the banks of the Ohio. As they talked over changes in the settlement during their absences little did either dream of the valiant fight the girl was to make to save Wetzel's life.

Wetzel spent the night at the Boggs' home in order to be on hand for a shooting match scheduled the following day. This form of entertainment was popular, since skill with the rifle was a highly valued accomplishment on the frontier. The best shots in the Ohio Valley appeared to

compete in the contest.   A tack head at 100 paces was the
mark at which these crack shots aimed.

Wetzel watched the others place bullets around the
mark, some even hitting the edge of the tack.   When asked
to shoot he declined.   The man had a sense of the dramatic
and waited until pleadings and sneers virtually forced him
to try a shot.   After much persuasion he stepped forward
and said, "This shot is for Lydia Boggs."

The crowd winked and looked at each other.   Wetzel
raised his heavy rifle.   All eyes were upon him.   The rifle
cracked and the referees hurried forward to see where the
ball had struck.   It had hit the tack in the center, giving
Lewis the prize without question.

Without wishing to question the veracity of the old-time
reporters who told about famous marksmen driving a tack
at 100 yards, we often wonder how big the heads of the
tacks were.   If any one with a modern improved rifle will
keep shooting until he hits a tack at 50 or even 25 yards
he will appreciate the skill required to do the stunt at twice
the distance with an old-time crude flint-lock.

This shooting match further enhanced Lewis in the eyes
of the fair Lydia, but with true Wetzel disregard for the
weakness of women he did not follow up his advantage,
but left his laurels to pursue the painted redmen through
the trackless forest.

These redmen paid no taxes and bought no clothes.
Their wants were few and easily satisfied, while their biggest problem was how to keep out of mischief.   This they
could not solve, as subsequent events reveal.   In the spring
of the year—it was the year 1786—plans for crops or business deals being no part of their simple lives, they put on
some war paint, crossed the Ohio at Mingo Bottom, which
is three miles below Steubenville, and launched a spring
drive.

High-priced wars and bureaucratic delay have been
criticized, but they had no place in the Indians' scheme of
things.   Redtape never restricted them nor lack of funds

restrained their activities. Their method was as direct as it was simple. They would sneak up to a settler's holdings, dispatch the inhabitants and disappear in the glades of the forest. This doubtless seemed to their simple minds the height of efficiency, whereas it was in reality the height of stupidity.

What the Indians lacked was organization and mass production. Killing settlers one or two at a time was too slow to stop the encroaching flood. Warfare on a small scale is unprofitable although spectacular. A person may catch fish one at a time on hook and line and have fun at it, but if he wants to keep a salmon canning factory supplied he must adopt other methods. So the net effect of the Indian's spring drive was negligible as far as destroying the white race is concerned, but it was most effective in stirring up armed resentment. The white folks did not like this individual destruction any more than they would have approved the wholesale method.

Stirred by the epidemic of raids settlers met at Wheeling to consider methods of protection. If the red brother insisted on a personal war they would accommodate him, so a subscription was drawn up offering $100 in cash to the scout who would first bring in an Indian's scalp. Fifty men shouted their readiness to try for this prize. Major McMahan was authorized to raise a company of twenty men. In half an hour his ranks were filled.

On the day of departure wives and children collected to see the expedition off. The "army" was lined up and counted. It contained twenty-one men—one too many.

"How is this?" asked the major.

"Wrong count," shouted a bystander.

"Right count," shouted another.

So the men counted off again, and there were 21. A woman cried, "Lydia's sweetheart is going and she's dressed to follow him." Whereupon Lydia stepped forward and denied the allegation.

Another bystander shouted, "The extra man is Dirty Dick."

A wild, long-haired, unkempt man covered with dust stepped from the ranks and said, "I could come no faster than I did. Let me go."

"Not so fast, my friend, not so fast," said the major.

"Let him go," shouted a dozen voices.

"Don't let him go," screamed a woman.

"Let him go," shouted Lydia Boggs.

"He makes more than 20 men," argued the first woman.

"Mind your own business, Mrs. Madison," retorted Lydia. From which conversation we assume that Bertha was still anxious about Wetzel's welfare and Lydia anxious for him to win more honor. What the major thought of all this free advice we are not informed, but army officers in the backwoods were not allowed to let their self-importance interfere with the democracy of the times.

"Hurrah for Lydia," shouted some of the settlers.

"Hurrah for Bertha Madison," shouted others.

Major McMahan turned to the stranger and asked, "Who are you?"

"I am Lewis Wetzel, Major."

"The company is twenty-one," boomed the major in a voice of authority. "Forward, March!" and the little party of scalp hunters set off toward the West.

On the other side of the river they picked up an Indian trail which they followed to the Muskingum River. Here they located a party of Indians around a new lodge on the bank of the river. The Indians outnumbered them, so the Whites held a conference to discuss the situation.

Wetzel sat alone on a log while the consultation was going on. The Whites decided to retreat. At the order to move Wetzel remained on his log. His companions argued with him to accompany them, but he only said, "Go on, you fools. I came out to fight Indians. I'm not going to run home with my fingers in my mouth." As the rest of the "army" marched toward home, following this bloodless war, Wetzel leaned idly against a tree until they were out of sight. When they disappeared his manner changed and he dived into the woods, slipping from tree to tree with the silence of a cat, every nerve alert, gun cocked, the perfect scout, master of his fate and fearing none, rejoicing in his skill and keen for the fray; lone defender of the settlements, going forward to meet the reds in numbers which had scared 20 men back to the shelter of their homes.

Through thorny underbrush, over piles of fallen tree tops, into bank-filled streams he pressed on, but nary an Indian did he see. Night came on, and it grew cold. Wet to the hide, even the hardy Wetzel was not comfortable. So he sought out a sheltered ravine, where behind some fallen trees he dug a little hole. In the bottom of this he built a fire, covering it loosely with leaves and dirt. '

This may not strike the reader as a pleasant way to ward off a spring cold, but it served Wetzel's purpose. He sat down on the ground, encircled the hole and fire with his legs, covered himself with his blanket, and thus hidden from the eyes of any wandering savage, baked the moisture out of his wet clothes and warmed his shivering bones. When well warmed up he chewed a little dried venison and corn, got a drink from a convenient spring and, spreading branches on the ground at the lee side of a fallen log, curled up and slept with a clear conscience.

The next day he was "up and at 'em" with the rising sun, but he roamed the forest until afternoon before encountering anything of interest. Then he was awarded for his persistency by coming suddenly on a vacant camp.

Two blankets and a kettle were there, which in the language of the forest told him that the camp's occupants were two Indians who planned to return when they had finished a day's hunt. So the tireless and patient Lewis hid and awaited their return.

When night descended the reds came, cooked a supper which smelled very good to the hungry scout. He let them eat it in peace, hoping that they would drop off to sleep and thus make his job easier. It is messy work to attack two live Indians at their meal, besides it might look like intruding. When they are safely asleep the pleasure of putting them out of their troubles is not marred by any thoughtless action on their part. But they did not go right to sleep. They laughed and talked, and were in high good humor.

It is a credit to the fortitude of Lewis that he had so much patience with them. We could hardly blame him if he had run up and given one a punch in the nose for keeping him awake so long. But Lewis was considerate and fought off the mosquitoes until one of the hunters picked up a burning brand from the fire and went out to surprise a buck at a deerlick. The other redman dropped asleep, and the white watcher knew his opportunity had come.

Disgusted at his bad luck in losing one victim Lewis crept toward the sleeping brave. When close enough with one stroke of his knife he separated the sleeper from his earthly cares, and sent him still dreaming to the Happy Hunting Ground. Securing the single scalp Wetzel headed for home. He made the trip in two days and delivered the trophy to Major McMahan at Wheeling.[73]

When McMahan offered Wetzel the $100 prize for the scalp, the scout refused the money saying that getting the scalp was his reward. However, later in the day he returned and stated that he would accept the money. It was given to him. The following day "Dirty Dick" was dispatched with a note to Lydia Boggs.

On the outside of the note was written: "For Lydia to buy housekeeping things with." Inside was the $100 sewed up in a leaf. "Dirty Dick" did not know Wetzel and could not tell Lydia who had sent the note, but she knew him and guessed correctly as to its dispatcher.

---

73.   Lewis Bonnett told Lyman C. Draper that this scalp hung in his father's upper chamber room for over two years. Bonnett to Draper, *Draper's Mss.*, 11E89 in the State Historical Society of Wisconsin, Madison, Wisconsin; also Samuel Hildreth's *"Pioneer History of America,"* and R. C. V. Myers *"Wetzel the Scout."*

Among the hardships of the present is the change in conditions. No longer can the bold warrior and shy lover collect the wherewithal to furnish a home by going out in the night and scalping a careless redskin. To-day he must earn the money in more prosaic fashion.

We are led to believe that this prize money was acceptable to the charming Lydia, but again the nodding historian fails to tell us whether Lewis followed up the good impression it made. Evidently not, for again we find him far from her arms and near the embrace of a sextet of villainous reds.

Thus tradition does not picture Lewis as much of a ladies' man. In fact the less said about his love affairs the better, since he seems much dumber with women than with Indians.

CHAPTER VIII

Lewis' Daring Deeds Among Indians as a Young Man

IT IS WITH the redskins that the story tellers delight to recount the tales of Lewis' daring. The one about him catching a half dozen braves has lived through all these years, and the wonder is that it has not grown bigger with the telling.

"Well, boy, we've got to get a fence around that wheat field," said honest John Wetzel hitting a knot in a length of fire-wood with a well-aimed shot of tobacco juice. "Stray horses, stray cattle and wild animals eat or tramp down every crop we try to grow there. You go split some rails and we'll fence 'em out."

Lewis Wetzel scowled as he pushed an oiled rag back and forth through his rifle barrel with the ramrod, but said, "Yes, sir." He was the bully of the Ohio Valley, but had a healthy respect for his father, so when John said "Go" Lewis went and asked no questions. The wild horses mentioned were the offspring of horses which escaped from settlers. Every year at fly time the horses showed a great dislike for the locality. They simply went away from there, crossing the mountains to the east or swimming the river to the west. Horseflies were to blame for some of the squabbling and fighting between whites and reds over ownership of horses, each claiming those which had left their homes to get away from the flies.

Shouldering an axe Lewis struck up the creek to a straight chestnut he knew would split easily. Soon chips were flying and the sounds of axe blows rang up and down the ravine. They reached the ears of a party of reds moving silently through the forest. The warriors stopped, listened a moment, looked significantly at each other and with one accord changed their course in the direction of the blows.

Lewis puffed away, delivering each stroke with energy. He had notched one side of the tree to the center and the axe blade was eating away at the other side when the chestnut trembled, tore at its mooring fibers and crashed to the ground in a cloud of dust and flying dead twigs.

The youth attacked the fallen tree with gusto, chopped it in two about 16 feet from the butt and started at one end to split it. With wedge and axe he opened a crack and was inserting another wedge to widen this opening when a cold shiver ran up his back. Animals and men in the wilds frequently have intuitions or promptings explained only as those of a "sixth sense".

Showing no excitement the rail-splitter looked up and beheld three Indians regarding him gravely. Glancing behind him he saw three others in like position. This situation meant quick thinking or the loss of the long black hair Lewis valued highly and which the Indians coveted earnestly. So completely was the boy trapped that the redskins saw an easy chance to capture him alive, which from their point of view was even more to be desired than to take his scalp and leave his body for the wolves. One of the braves informed the white man that he was to go with them. He said he would be glad to accommodate them, but pointed to the log and said it would have to be split first, and that the sooner that was done the sooner they could be on their way.

In order to hurry this job Wetzel suggested that the Indians help him. This evidently appealed to their sense of humor, for they readily assented. Lewis showed them how to arrange themselves, three on each side of the log, grasping it in the crevice and pulling as he drove the wedge deeper. When the six had their fingers inserted deep in the crack with one blow of his axe Wetzel drove the wedge flying out. The log pinched together and held the six Indians as in a vise.

The rest of this log-splitting bee consisted of tomahawking and scalping six trapped reds and going home with the evidence of a half day's work.

John Wetzel, Sr., and his sons, Martin, Lewis, George and two other men whose last names were Scott and Miller, were returning from the Wetzel farm near Middlebourne, in Tyler County, W. Va., in June, 1786. They were attacked by the Indians two miles above Fish Creek and ordered to land on the Ohio shore. This they refused to do and the Indians fired on them, wounding John, Sr., mortally, and shooting his son George through the body and the same bullet that went through George's body killed a dog that was in the canoe. George told the others to lay down in the canoe for, "I am a dead man anyhow". They all did so but Lewis and he kept firing at the Indians until they were out of gun shot. Another bullet from the Indians' guns went through the side of the canoe, lodged against Martin's shoulder, cut a hole in his shirt, left a dent in the flesh that turned black, but did not have force enough to enter. John Wetzel, Sr., died soon after landing on the Virginia side of the river, and George[74] succumbed that night. They were buried side by side on the bank of Grave Yard Run near Baker's Station in Franklin District, Marshall County, W. Va., in coffins made of hickory bark.

A common sandstone marked the graves, bearing the inscriptions: "J. W. 1787; G. W. 1787".[75] In recent years the stones have been broken and carried away piece by

74. Another version says that George Wetzel was killed in 1782 while on a trapping expedition down to the Muskingum, and was buried in the sand at the head of Middle Island. The above is the true account. George Wetzel to Lyman C. Draper. *Draper's Mss.*, 24S50 and 20S79 in the State Historical Society of Wisconsin, Madison, Wisconsin.

75. This is an error, as *Settlement Book 1*, p. 35, Ohio County Records in the Courthouse at Wheeling, W. Va., gives the appraisement of John Wetzel's personal property as of August 19, 1786. See Appendices for details.

piece, until none remains to mark the place. The largest piece of known stone is said to be in a museum in Philadelphia.

The slaying of John Wetzel was a serious error on the redskins' part. While they had destroyed another white man they had further incensed one of their fiercest enemies. The high respect and affection in which Lewis Wetzel held his father now fanned into fiercer heat his hatred of the killers. He had lived up to his boyish oath, but from the time of his father's death he was more industrious than ever in his real trade or occupation, that of hunting savages. He and his brothers now hunted for sport and vengeance.

Lewis Wetzel stayed at Baker's Station for a few days after the death of his father and brother George. The next day he found two Indians near Baker's Station, who had a white woman prisoner. They were in the path ahead of Wetzel, and he shot the one he thought was an Indian; but he killed the white woman instead, as the Indian had taken the bonnet from her head and put it on his own to keep off the rain.[76]

Wetzel pursued the Indians to their camp, killed one, and two more took after him, he turned and shot one Indian dead and the other shot Wetzel through the thigh while he was reloading as he ran. The wound was only a flesh wound and did not stop Wetzel. As soon as he had his gun reloaded he shot the other Indian but only wounded him and he escaped.

Wetzel scalped the two Indians, marked the trees with his tomahawk where this fight occurred, and five days after his father and brother's death he appeared at Lewis Bonnett's home on Wheeling Creek with two scalps. Lewis Bonnett said, "I remember the day that we received the word my Uncle John Wetzel and my cousin George had been killed by the Indians. My father was raising a horse

---

76. This is the only time that Lewis Wetzel ever killed a woman, either White or red, and of course, this was a mistake about which he felt very badly.

stable at the time the news came. Jacob and John, Jr.,
Wetzel were at the raising."[77]

Years passed. The wandering Lewis Wetzel roamed up
and down the Ohio, branching off to right and left, living off
the country and carrying his private war into the enemies'
territory. This was a highly technical operation. One mistake and the annals of the frontier would have been short-
ened. But Wetzel was a thorough workman. He made no
mistakes, at least none which landed him at the stake.

He was not forgotten, either, by the lively young lady
for whom he had driven the tack and taken the scalp, nor
by the military authorities, whom he had so boldly flaunted.
Both hoped to catch him in the end.

After an absence of some time he showed up at Wheeling, and lived for awhile with his brothers and sisters and
his uncle, Lewis Bonnett. He also stayed with a friend,
Mrs. George Crookis. He was respected by the public, for
while the need for the protection of such men as he had
not vanished his type was becoming scarce. With the
growth of the settlement and the coming of more people
from the East, greedy for the free, simple land of the West,
the character of the border was changing from the rough
and ready, half-wild scout type to the more serious workers,
the white-handed gentry, the wealthy and cultivated. In
place of the cabin and the clearing little industries were
springing up.

The Indian backed off, defiant, revengeful and crafty
but helpless, before the steady advance of civilization. In-
dividually he might feel that he could cope with the Whites,
but in the face of this mass movement he knew he was
doomed. The place had become so quiet that Wetzel was
pointed out to strangers and his exploits recounted. But
Indians or no Indians in evidence things were not to remain
in a state of quietude with Wetzel around.

---

77. An old man named Wiser told Dr. Hildreth this story in
1786. Bonnett to Draper, *Draper's Mss.*, 11E23 and 11E30 in the
State Historical Society of Wisconsin, Madison, Wisconsin.

Gossip said he had returned in 1788 to see his sisters and his sweetheart Lydia Boggs. It is certain he did not return to see his mother; if he did he had a queer way of showing his affection for her.

"I am sorry mother is not here to see you," ventured one of his sisters timidly. "She was never strong after father's death and we had quite a time to get her over it. She often spoke of you and the other boys, but she thinks it rather hard she should be left alone without a son in her old days. She needs someone to console her."

"She has someone now, I have heard," interrupted the son.

"She has gone up the river for a spell to visit—"

"Her sweetheart's people," he interrupted again. "Yes, I understand. But I did not come to see her. She is nothing to me. I have no mother. She forgot my father and now has a new lover."

"She is lonely," defended the sister.

"Had she not her children?" demanded Lewis.

"She had grown weak and querulous," said the girl.

"And will marry again in consideration of her weakness and querulousness?" replied Lewis. "Let it be so. My mother was a strong woman who helped to make a home for her children in the wilderness. She died with my father. She is better without me. She has a sweetheart to take care of her. I could never like her friend so I will not wait to see him. Good-bye, my sister."

"But indeed, Lewis, he is not a foolish man," said one of the sisters. "He is even trying to find out the cause of the turkey-call and has left mother with his family while he is away."

"Turkey call?" inquired Lewis, interested at last.

"You know what I mean. The call that annoys us so much now," replied the girl.

Before we judge our hero too hastily let us remember that the emotions of the border people were not worn for public exhibition. It was easier for them to express their hardihood in warlike pastimes than to show affection in a way that might be construed into weakness. It is possible that the knowledge of his mother's second love together with his deep regard for his father, made him assume a harsh, indifferent attitude he did not really feel. However, in view of the absence of any consideration for the woman who carried him across the Alleghenies we can find little to excuse him for leaving her unprotected and then criticizing her for considering a second marriage.

So Lewis went to call on Lydia Boggs, who was more interesting to him than his mother. He asked her about the turkey-call and about his mother's love. Lydia told him that his mother's friend was a sensible, practical man.

"Then why will he marry my mother?" the model son questioned himself. He could not understand it, but he could understand the turkey-call which had mystified the settlement.

Lydia explained to him that a weird cry as birds in distress flying overhead had aroused all the superstitious fear of the people. They thought it a harbinger of evil, some saying it meant punishment for the country that had rebelled against the king. People in their houses at night shuddered as they listened to the cry of the birds.

Men from the fort went out across the fields to find this evil bird of the night — and never returned. The cries seemed to come up from the earth, down from the sky; they were heard in the midst of gatherings; women alone in their homes trembled at them; they awoke folks at night. Now near, now far, the wailing sounds brought terror to strong hearts.

All sorts of stories were told about them. One young wife said that at noon, while rocking her baby to sleep she heard the strange bird's cry come from the cradle, and that night the child died.

Another woman, old and bedridden, awoke in the night and saw in the far-off hill what she called a "death light," from which the frightful cry floated over to her in ghastly warning. Everybody had heard the cry and was anxious to tell about it. Some young women became hysterical in their excited recitals about this "witchcraft". Thus on Wetzel's tour of inquiry he got plenty of information about the strange noise; one account says he was told fifty stories in as many minutes.

These wild accounts led Wetzel to believe that something more substantial than spirits was back of the cries which were frightening the people. He therefore determined to do a little private investigating.

Evening finds him out in the hills and up in a tree, where he spent the night reposing in a crotch. From this cramped but commanding position he heard at long intervals throughout the night the unearthly cries of which he had been told. Sometimes they were faint and far away; again at his very feet. Once he heard the brush rustle beneath him, as if stirred by some passing agency. Then sad and gruesome rose the wail, to die away in a foreboding stillness. Again the soft rustling of bushes. Straining his eyes as he would he could detect no bird or animal.

In the east a glint of silver showed, and then the yellow moon peeped over the hills to see what this uncanny racket was all about. Paths of silver stretched over the forest floor as the moonbeams penetrated the dense shadows. Gluing his eye to a silver streak the ever vigilant Wetzel beheld a strange apparition.

Out of the black shadows and across the moonlight path slipped a long, many linked body — or was it a chain of bodies? Into the black shadows again slipped this fearsome being. And as it passed silently up toward the crest of the hill once more the weird cry arose from the heart of the wilderness and seemed to float along the path of silver and down to the inhabitants of the pioneer village.

Turning his eyes toward the settlement Lewis saw lights moving as the worried inmates wandered around in their homes, seeking an answer to the cries.

"I am glad my mother's friend is more practical," said the watcher in the tree.

At the first break of dawn the sounds ceased. Wetzel descended from his perch and examined the brush below. The place was trodden here and there. Down on his knees he examined the crushed grass. "It is as I expected," he said.

He followed the trail up the hill. It led him sixty feet

Cave and rock where Wetzel killed the turkey-call Indian in 1788, as it appears today. Note hole through which the Indian's head appeared.

above the water on the east side of Creek Hill, and there ended. Beating around he found the mouth of a cavern, its entrance almost hidden by dense foliage and vines.

Concealing himself in this wild growth he waited. All forenoon he hid there, and nothing happened. Once he thought something came from the cave's mouth, but hidden as he was he could not see the entrance, and there was no sound. All the afternoon he waited. Wetzel was a good waiter. He never got tired and gave up the watch, on this or other occasions of the kind. Late in the day he was rewarded by again hearing the mysterious sound. A weird turkey-cry cut the silence of the woods. It was followed by another and another, until it seemed as if a whole brood of birds were in agony.

The cries came from the cavern. Cautiously raising up Lewis looked over the tall grass until he could see the cave's entrance, but not a leaf or twig stirred. The patient watcher watched on. At last the tangled vines at the cavern's mouth trembled, then were still. Again they were agitated, and from their midst stretched forth a hand. "Not a dead devil," thought the faithful watcher.

The hand pushed aside some vines and the twisted tuft of a redskin arose from the opening. A villainously painted face appeared and looked to right and left. The mouth twisted into a "long hornlike shape" and the long wailing cry rent the air. The head disappeared as if by magic.

"Not a dead devil," said the watcher again.

After the Indian's head disappeared Wetzel looked down the hill and saw three or four white men approaching, searching the bushes as they came. He could hear what they said.

"It was around here," said one.

"Do you think it was a bird or a spirit?" asked another.

"No doubt of it," responded the first. "It is a spirit."

"That must be my mother's lover," thought Lewis grimly. "My father would never have spoken thus."

"If I had thought it was a spirit I would not have come after it with a rifle," spoke a third for the first time. "Nor had I if I had thought it was a turkey either. Wetzel is not an Indian murderer, but this is an Indian ruse."

"You mean Lewis Wetzel?" inquired one of the party.

"Yes, I am going to marry John Wetzel's widow, his mother."

Wetzel turned his attention toward the cave, ready with cocked gun. This time he did not have long to wait. Up from the tangled vines poked a gun barrel, then a scalp-lock. Again the weird note sounded through the air. As the uncanny sound sped toward the valley Lewis took a fine aim at the polished head. The deadly rifle spoke, just as the Indian raised his own gun at the Whites below. A curl of smoke, and the dreadful cry was silenced permanently.

"A dead devil," said Wetzel, as the vines sprang back over the form that fell in their midst.

"That was a rifle shot," said the foremost of the Whites, hurrying toward the sound. "It means something."

"Might it not be a decoy?" asked another. All paused.

"Even if it is we might as well look into it," spoke the man who was going to marry John Wetzel's widow.

They then plunged forward.

Wetzel got to the mouth of the cave without the Whites seeing him. He pressed down the vines from its entrance so that the Indian lay in full view. A yard from the redman lay the body of a settler.

"They will understand," said the scout. He turned away, hesitated and returned. "Can I or can I not?" he asked himself. He could see the manly figure of his mother's friend breaking his way across the stubble. "Never mind. I do not know him. I cannot know him. He may not be a coward, but he cannot take the place of my father—with me. But my mother shall not be a widow at the hands of the redskins a second time. Poor mother." He plunged into the tall grass and hid from the approaching strangers.

The Whites came up and startled when they saw the dead Indian.

"This explains it all," one said.

"Who fired the shot?" asked another.

The others turned over the dead body. "Here is one of Lewis Wetzel's bullets," said one, holding up something between thumb and finger. "It went straight through the Indian's head."

On hearing this Wetzel departed without making himself known to the Whites. He had not only avenged his father's death, saved the life of his mother's second lover, but he had turned the trick in approved style and knew that he would get credit for it.   For Lewis was an artist. He did not do his work in bungling fashion, but finished every enterprise with a flourish and with due regard for dramatic effect.   As far as his affection for his mother's friend is concerned, it is said that Lewis never saw his mother's sweetheart again.[78]

Another Story of A Gobbler Indian In Belmont County, Ohio

"For several winters in turkey time, the people around the fort at Wheeling had been plagued by an Indian who would station himself on the Ohio side of the river and call so much like a wild turkey that no one could tell the difference. The people at the fort called him the 'Gobbler Indian'."

On the 12th day of January 1783, or old Christmas, which was always punctually kept at the fort we had two large turkeys roasted, and a lot of twelfth-day cake baked. Twelfth-day cake is made of unleavened dough, slightly sweetened with spice, cloves and cinnamon bark worked in it, and baked in a Dutch oven like a loaf of light bread.   It was baked a day or two before and eaten cold.   When we were killing the turkeys, Lewis Wetzel had the feet of one cut off up where the feathers come on, and the wings at the first joint before it was scalded.   These he put away carefully in his hunting bag.   After dinner he took a drumstick bone, punched a hole in the joint ends and then fixed a piece of quill staved down thin in the big end.   These he put away with the other things.   In a few days the sun shone strong, melting the snow, except on the north side of the hills and ridges.   The night was cold and froze the ground hard.   The next morning an hour or two before day, Lewis Wetzel got up, took his rifle and hunting bag, swung them

78.   From R. C. V. Myer's, "Wetzel the Scout."

over his shoulder and left the fort. The rest I will tell you as he told me:

"I crossed the river, went up the north side of the hill to the top of the ridge, and came back on the ridge about a half a mile. It was now good daylight. I went as carefully as I could down to where the snow was still on, and made some tracks along its edge with my turkey feet. I then came on down the ridge within a hundred yards of where I intended to hide myself. I then sighted along the upper edge of the snow in a straight line to my hiding place, and wherever there was snow on that line I made turkey tracks, toes east, but clear of the snow with my own feet. When I got within twenty steps of my place to hide, the ground was raised a little and there was some snow. I here made tracks as near as I could like a turkey does when it is about to fly to roost. I then fixed the wings and flapped them in the snow. I now went back a hundred yards or more and crossed down on the south side of the ridge, and came back to the river. I then went up the point of the ridge to my hiding place. I took my drumsticks and began to call like a turkey. In a little while my call was answered and presently a large Indian came in sight and was leaning down and going to and fro, as if hunting a trail. I kept on calling; he answered and came on towards me. I now examined my priming, and rubbed the frizzen and flint with a piece of punk, to be sure of my shot. By this time he had got to the little raise, looked down and gave a grunt; then looked about up in the trees, and then down at the tracks again. He kept moving so that I was afraid to shoot for fear I would miss. He now lifted his gun in his left hand, turned it sideways and struck it with his right. He then stood still and looked right towards me. I pulled on him. He threw up his hands, trembled and fell backwards. I knew that it was his last sickness. He did not get his turkey this time, and you will not be plagued with this, 'Gobbler Indian' any more. I gave one of my yells which was my way and came back to the fort with his scalp in my hunting bag."[79]

The Wetzel luck was good, but not perfect. Even this alert and cautious scout could be caught napping. How it happened we do not know, but one night following the turkey-call experiences Indians captured Lewis. Here was a prize, indeed. The most famous and ferocious of their foes delivered into their hands. It was an occasion for celebration and ceremony.

Like Lewis the Indians were also artists in their lines. They took pride in their calling, and were not indifferent to the applause of their home folks. It would have been a simple matter to kill the captive and bear his long-haired scalp home in triumph, but what would the warriors' wives and sweethearts say? Public opnion and personal pride demanded that the arch enemy of the redman be presented in living stature for his foes to gaze upon, and then to wreak vengeance on.

The white man was guarded day and night as his captors moved toward their Sandusky towns. No chance appeared for the cunning Wetzel to contrive an escape. So assiduous was his guard that he reached the Indian village alive.

A meeting was held to determine his fate.

It was gleefully suggested by the Indians that Lewis be burned alive, meanwhile subjected to the leisure tortures so dear to the heart of the redskin. However, one old chief arose and asked the privilege of adopting the captive. He argued that Wetzel was too good a fighter to be killed. And here the Wetzel luck returned.

If adopted he would add renown to the tribe, pleaded the old chief. Many warriors have fallen before his rifle and tomahawk, countered others. And thus the primitive

---

79. *R. H. Taneyhill's History, of Belmont County, Ohio* contains this episode as it was given to him by Joshua Davis of Belmont county, Ohio. Davis had known Lewis Wetzel and while younger than Wetzel had done some scouting with him, as mentioned in footnote 70.

trial went on. The outcome of the pow-wow was that
Wetzel must pay for his sins by dying the next day. He
was bound hand and foot, a guard placed to watch him
while the tribe eagerly awaited the morrow with its ceremonies. It was the judgment of the majority and there was
no appeal.

But the old chief was not satisfied with this decision
and determined to take justice in his own hands. He did
not want to see this great fighter roasting at the stake.
So in the stillness of the night the redman crept through
the rear of the shack where the captive was held, cut the
thongs which bound him and led him out into the woods.
There he gave Wetzel his son's rifle, ammunition, and knife.
Mounting a horse the Indian led the rescued prisoner toward the Ohio River. At the Muskingum the old Indian
stopped. "Good-bye," said he. And Lewis Wetzel, hero of
the border, turned and shot his rescuer dead. So much for
pioneer gratitude, or was it a streak of madness in this
Teuton's blood, which explains his savagery on this and
other occasions?

"He made me walk, and he was nothing but an Indian,"
was Wetzel's explanation when he turned up at an Ohio
settlement with a fresh scalp at his belt.[80]. His explanation
may have seemed sufficient to himself, but it did not advance him in the estimation of certain plain-spoken women,
who let him know in no uncertain terms what they thought
of such pay for his rescue. Lydia Boggs defended him.
Whether he appreciated her loyalty we do not know, but
this was not the last time that she came to his rescue.

No man on the border dared say a word. We are told

---

80. Thomas Ewing wrote in the *Belmont Chronicle* January 26,
1871, in relating this story of Lewis Wetzel, that he had been shot
at so many times by the Indians and missed that the Indians thought
Wetzel was always in a spell. Lewis Wetzel was superstitious and
always put a piece of silver in his bullets as a magic to keep the
Indians' bullets from hitting him or the Indians from capturing him.
The magic failed sometimes, as in theis case. Lewis Wetzel was known
by the Indians as "Old Deathwind," because he could run so fast and
so long and he sometimes called his rifle "old-dare-devil" and "old-kill-
nigger."

they agreed with Lydia that he was no murderer. But probably in private they held different opinions, for he became so thoroughly ostracized that he left the country, going down to Kentucky, where this contradictory character in a measure redeemed himself.

Did the savage heart hide finer thought never yet brought to light, or has tradition, sickened by his monotonous slaughter, painted a pretty picture of the man to atone for its gruesome delight in his killings? Or did outraged public opinion knock some sense into this strange mind? We cannot say. All we know is that down in Kentucky Lewis Wetzel was a changed man.

Living around Limestone and Washington, Ky., he took part in hunting parties, helped harvest the grain and cut trees for winter firewood. He voiced opposition to making women captives. "Not a woman," he would say, "for our mothers are women." The reader will here recall his solicitude for his own mother!

"Our fathers are men too," he was told.

"Men can defend themselves," said Lewis. "But men to attack and capture women that is not for me. That is for you."

It should be recalled that we have no record of Wetzel ever, either before or after his capture by the Indians, injuring a woman of any color intentionally. In view of his feeling toward the redmen it is also strange that the only kindness he ever showed to any woman, with the possible exception of Lydia Boggs, was toward one of the hated race.

An Indian girl about fifteen years old was brought into a woods camp. She had had the privilege of seeing her three brothers and her father shot by the white men who brought her into the camp where the scouts were assembled. Some of these gallant specimens of depravity complimented the girl on her appearance and she turned away abashed by their rudeness.

"Let us make a vivandiere of her, such as the French have," suggested a young man.

"Let the girl go," commanded a stern voice.

"Who spoke in that tone?" demanded the young fellow, leaping up in anger.

Lewis Wetzel came up to him and putting his hand on the boy's shoulder said, "I spoke, lad. The girl must go. Have you sisters? If you have, think of their position in an Indian camp."

"Their position in such a place should make me detain this girl from revenge," said the lad.

"It should make you liberate her from pity," said the scout quietly. Walking over to the girl he said, "Go, child. Your people's camp is waiting for you."

The Indian maiden broke into tears and would not be quieted. The rough men who a few minutes ago were cruel and callous about her fate, gathered around in solicitude, trying to make her stop crying. Those tears were weapons they were not prepared to resist.

The girl peeped through her fingers and saw only sympathy on the rough faces before her. A smile flashed through her tears and two black eyes softened as they gazed in affection at her stalwart rescuer. Obeying her impulse she ran up to Wetzel, caught his hand in both of hers and covered it with kisses. Here was a predicament for the Indian and woman hater, and the girl did not help him out of it, for she refused to be separated from him.

"Indian girl got no father, no brothers," said the maiden. "She like white brave; she go with him."

"But the white brave cannot take you," said Lewis kindly, as he always spoke to children.

"Pooh," said the squaw. "Indian girl don't want to be took. She take herself. She know every path. She follow after white brave." Retaining her hold on Lewis Wetzel's hand she seemed willing and capable of carrying out her promise.

"What am I to do with her?" asked the embarrassed scout. This was fun for the other Whites, who appreciated the situation of the man, who was master of every occasion in which Indians were concerned, now at sea before a weak and insignificant member of that race. Getting no help from them the scout took the girl and they went through the woods until they came to an encampment of her people. Here the foxy Wetzel intimated that he wanted a conference with the redmen, so asked the girl to prepare the way for him.

Glad to serve him she sprang forward. When he saw her safe within the line of Indian pickets he dived through the underbrush and departed from that vicinity. But the native child was not to be shoved aside so easily. That night she walked into the white men's camp.

"What shall I do with her?" asked one of the men.

"Do you think this girl was allowed to come because she wanted to?" demanded Wetzel. "She is either a decoy, or her people cast her off, now that her father and brothers are no more."

"Her people cast her off—" The voice came from the darkness. "Because she loves white man." The crack of a rifle accompanied the last word, and the little girl, who had done no wrong, but who was not wanted by either her own or her enemies' people, crumpled, lifeless at Wetzel's feet.

Instantly the camp was in an uproar. Men deployed in all directions seeking the murderer. The search was in vain. By midnight all had gathered in camp again. There in the witching hour the rough and ready border men, who would have as soon scalped a redskin as chop a chicken's head off, dug a grave for the young victim they had made an orphan and who had touched their hearts.

No pomp and circumstance, no funeral trappings or ceremony to sooth the grief of bereaved relatives, no relatives, no banks of flowers or hymns of supplication, no timed chant of priest or exposition of preacher, but to the chorus of gathering wolves the Indian girl was wrapped in a blanket and laid in a gloomy narrow trench.

As the men were about to throw on the earth Wetzel

stopped them. "We commit this body to the earth from whence it came," said the fiddle-playing warrior in a slow voice. "As from the earth spring up flowers and healthful things for man's life, so may this immortal soul arise to the seat of mercy, a flower, a fruit, in the sight of God. Amen." He motioned for the men to proceed, and earth soon covered the breast of the wild flower so suddenly crushed under the trampings of two contending races.

A fire was made over the new grave to protect it from wolves. When the flames leaped high the white men moved silently away and made a new camp from which a rising golden vapor could be seen marking the resting place of the redman's child.

When morning came Wetzel went alone to the grave and stood long in contemplation as he gazed at the white ashes. Arousing himself with a sigh, he looked around and seeing that he was alone, plucked scarlet blossoms that grew nearby and strewed them on the ashes until the ground was carpeted as with sunset.

The girl had died as he might have died, or as he might have killed his sister if she had chosen an Indian for protector. What was the difference? What was the difference between the soul of an Indian and that of a white man? Perhaps for the first time in his life this question came to him. The little red girl had done more than all the warriors of her race, or all the authority of the Whites; she had raised a perplexing question in a one-track mind.[81]

On one occasion Captain Samuel Brady and Lewis Wetzel joined forces in a call on the Indians of Ohio. Both could speak the Delaware and the Shawnee tongues. Painting their faces in the prevailing style and assuming the garb of the tribesmen they strolled serenely into the village of the foeman. Each in other tight places had played Indian so well as to fool their foes and save their hair. Wetzel was able to deceive his hosts but Brady's blue eyes gave

---

81. From R. C. V. Myer's, *"Wetzel the Scout."*

him away. The Indians attacked the spies with great enthusiasm, but the latter shot and clubbed their way out, leaped on a pair of horses and galloped through the timber. On they raced without slackening speed until one of the horses gave out. Both mounted the remaining one and urged it until it, too, could go no farther. Leaving this horse they eventually secured a third and finally reached the Ohio river.

Brady rode the horse over and Wetzel swam. He had great endurance, but this swim in icy water following the violent exertions nearly finished him. It was so cold that water froze on his body. Exhausted and all but frozen, Wetzel could travel no longer. They killed and disemboweled the horse and stuffed Wetzel inside to keep him alive while Brady built a fire to thaw them out.[82]

Jonathan Zane and Lewis Wetzel Kill Five Indians

Jonathan Zane and Lewis Wetzel were once returning home from hunting Zane's horses when passing through some high weeds near the bank of the Ohio river at a spot within the present limits of the City of Wheeling. Not far from the fort they saw five Indians jump into the stream and swim for the island, in the Ohio opposite the fort. They quickly took aim at two of the savages, fired, and the Indians sank. Loading and firing in quick succession two more were killed before reaching the opposite bank. The fifth and last one, seeing the fate of his companions, concealed himself behind a "sawyer", near the shore of the island. The effort to see him was about to be abandoned, when the scouts noticed a small portion of his body protruding from the log. Drawing a fine sight on their rifles,

---

82. From Cecil B. Hartley's *"Life of Samuel Brady,"* 1860.

both were discharged at the same time, and the fifth savage
floated down the river.[83]

---

83.   Jonathan Zane was the father of Catharine, Eliza, Cynthia,
Sally, Hannah, Nancy, Isaac, Asa and Benjamin Zane.   Jonathan
Zane was born in Berkeley County, Virginia, and came with his
brother Ebenezer Zane, to Wheeling in 1769.   He also made exploring
expeditions with another brother, Silas Zane, up and down the Ohio,
and was the most experienced hunter of his day in the frontier country.   He rendered valuable service as a spy.   He was a guide in the
Wakatomica campaign of 1774.   He also accompanied Brodhead in
the same capacity in the expedition against the Munsies and Senecas
in 1779, in which he was wounded.   Jonathan was again one of the
guides in the campaign of Crawford against Sandusky; also a con-
fidential advisor of the commander.
   If Jonathan Zane's advice had been followed the terrible calamity
that befell the unfortunate expedition would have been averted, as
he told them that the enemy were very numerous and would defeat
them.   *History of the Panhandle,* by J. H. Newton, 1879.

CHAPTER IX

Lewis' Capture and Trial at Fort Harmar

JAMMED between the desperate and unsubmissive Indian race on one side and the determined and unconquered Caucasian race on the other, the inhabitants of the border land had little time to weigh the niceties of human conduct or indulge in philosophical introspection. To them life was primitive. At every turn not only the welfare but the very existence of their families was at stake. The young government at Washington had its hands full with new and unexpected problems. Its citizens on the edge of civilization must be left to shift for themselves. That they held their own and secured a foothold without machines or capital is as remarkable as that they clung to the principles of justice in their dealings with each other, and in a large way with the Indians.

It was a war to the finish, a time that produced such men as Lewis Wetzel, who was steadfast in his purpose, and whose greatest fault was too much zeal in the work he felt called on to do. This zeal aroused the admiration of the enemy, but was sometimes embarrassing to the broader minded Whites, who looked forward to peace.

The officers under General Harmar had standing orders to arrest Lewis Wetzel as "the murderer of the peaceful Indian." Wherever he went the shadow of his crime followed, although so far behind that it caused him no particular inconvenience. In fact such was the state of public opinion and fears that it is questionable whether his reputation was not enhanced rather than harmed by the accusation.

One of Wetzel's outstanding characteristics was an almost incredible patience. He could wait all night, crouched

in the shelter of a protecting bush, to deal summary vengeance on a group of sleeping Indians when they arose in
the morning. He could wait all day perched up in a
tree to quiet a disturbing "turkey-call". But authority
is also patient. Its patience is not a matter of hours or
days, but of weeks and months, yes, years if necessary.

General Harmar went about his duties and left his order
for Lewis Wetzel's capture to take care of itself. In order to
hasten the event it was suggested that a reward be placed
on the scout's head. But public opinion, formed in fear of
Indians, again interposed. The General declined to offer a
reward, knowing that it would make the settlers indignant
and obstruct rather than hasten the arrest of his man.
Thus biding his time, and relying on secrecy and chance
to land his game, the General pursued the course least likely
to give offense and most likely to place Lewis Wetzel in his
hands. The scout, undoubtedly, had dismissed the matter
from his mind, since to him the so-called crime must have
seemed a slight offense.

Down in Kentucky Lewis took no pains to keep under
cover and was seated on a bench in a bar-room playing his
"fiddle" when a couple of soldiers strolled into the room.
They were part of a detachment which was going down the
Ohio River and had stopped at Limestone for rest and re-
freshment.

The long-haired, husky scout played on, sensing no
danger. He was 26 years old at the time, of athletic build,
especially muscular in arms and shoulders. His carefully
braided hair knotted around his shoulders when combed out
would reach nearly to the calves of his legs. He was on
the tall order, small head, black eyes and piercing in the
extreme, a long spare face, high cheek bones, a swarthy
complexion, occasioned in a great measure by his exposure
to the sun, and very much pitted by smallpox; had his ears
bored and wore silk tassels in them at times or some other
ornament; active on his feet, his legs well proportioned,
feet on the small order. A penetrating mind, sound judg-

ment in regard to Indian encounters, and a plan once laid nothing could deter him from putting it into execution; smart and active in all his movements, and a noted marksman. He could shoot and aim well; a strong constitution, and was blessed with remarkably good health; no education, not capable of keeping his own journal, which is a great pity. He could not write his name.[84]

Thus he was a picturesque figure. His reputation as a fearless scout and energetic warrior did not suffer on close examination.

As the soldiers looked this striking figure over their appetite for official approval at the expense of a personal encounter disappeared, and they quietly left the room. Outside they hurriedly told their comrades of Wetzel's presence. One by one the company then sauntered into the bar-room. The fiddler played on. These newcomers were white men, and he was suspicious only of reds. Suddenly at a signal twenty men jumped on him. Lewis Wetzel was prisoner again.

That night Lieutenant Lawler delivered the captured man to General Harmar at Cincinnati.

"So, Wetzel, we meet again," said the general. "This time you will not have the chance to reward my clemency so vilely. Your irons will be doubly strong, and you must become used to a lack of exercise."

News spread through the valley that Lewis Wetzel was a prisoner, to be tried for the murder of an Indian at Fort Harmar. On hearing about it frontiersmen condemned the government for understanding so little about Indian warfare. The crime, to them, was that Lewis Wetzel should be arrested, not that an Indian had been killed. The latter was an achievement, not a crime.

If the General did not forget Lewis neither did the lad's girl friend Lydia Boggs. His absence as a sort of voluntary

---

84. From letter of Lewis Bonnett to Lyman Draper, Jan.24, 1849. *Draper's Mss.* 11E89 in the State Historical Society of Wisconsin, Madison, Wisconsin.

exile in Kentucky had not erased from her mind memories of that stroll along the moon-lit Ohio. And like many another woman she came to the rescue of her mistreated lover with all the ferocity of her vital nature.

Lydia personally took charge of a campaign to set Lewis free. She went from settler to settler begging assistance. Through her tireless and timely efforts a conspiracy was formed to rescue the prisoner and massacre the garrison at Cincinnati. Lydia was up in arms. What could a puny army of men do against this militant woman?

Petitions for Wetzel's release poured in on the stubborn General. A scout sent by Lydia reported to Harmar that frontiersmen would wipe out the fort, troops and whole settlement if the prisoner were not set free. Some of Wetzel's more conservative friends tried to secure a writ of *habeas corpus.* But all these efforts failed. The General had his man, and he proposed to make him stand trial.

The hour of trial arrived. The prisoner was brought before the military court. "Speak, Wetzel," said the prosecutor. "Are you guilty, or not guilty?"

With folded arms Lewis faced his accuser.

"Guilty of what?" he asked.

"Of murdering a fellow being in cold blood, without provocation.''

"I killed an Indian. That is my crime," said Wetzel in a tone one might use if accused of killing a grasshopper. Of arguments pro and con, of lawyers' tricks or legal delays history is silent. We are not even told whether Lewis was tried before a jury. However, tradition says the judge delivered an opinion, in which he quoted liberally from the Scriptures, and showed that to Lewis' mind slaying the redman at Marietta was not a sin, but that some of the greatest crimes in history were due to acts not considered by the actors as wrong. Therefore it was useless to try to tell him that the act under consideration was not cold-blooded murder.

Lewis Wetzel was ordered to arise and receive his sentence, which was that he was "to hang by the neck until dead."

One of the condemned man's friends said, "He shall never die by hanging. We will rescue him or die ourselves."

The faithful Lydia refused to accept the verdict. Meetings were held and protests made. The weight of opinion was that the scout must be freed. "Not that he is Lewis Wetzel," they said, "but because our principle is involved. The man shall not hang. We shall see who has the strongest arm, this military law that presumes to teach us our duties toward a miscreant race who murder and pillage us with impunity, or we who own the land and have gained it inch by inch from just such foul thieves as this savage that Wetzel killed for us."

For a while the General paid little heed to these mutterings. "They are the protests of friends and others who are doing it to please Lydia Boggs and are natural in any case of a criminal condemned," he thought. But then the idea gained ground that it was not Lydia or Lewis but the principle involved which so aroused the settlers. This was a different matter.

If a man were to be hanged for killing an Indian, society would go to the dogs, reasoned the settlers. No man's property would be assured to him by law or justice. Lewis Wetzel represented themselves. His fate represented the retention or slipping away of the property they had gained through struggle and difficulties. Their position was shaky enough at best, and they could see no virtue in anything which would endanger it.

Before we condemn the settlers as being too greedy or unmerciful let us think of what so-called highly civilized nations do in similar cases. They do not slay a lone Indian but thousands of inhabitants for a little strip of soil. The settlers were obeying the first law of nature, which is self-preservation. The General represented organized government, and stood for law and order. Both equally right in their stand, and both victims not of personal ambition but of racial struggle for supremacy. They were simply pushed out in front to take the bumps; the force and responsibility was far behind them.

While the settlers were thus making an issue of the Wetzel affair and working themselves up in a rage of righteous indignation the redskins were taking advantage of the lax guarding by pilfering herds and gardens. But the Reds did not dare show themselves. They heard about the trial and the resultant public resentment, so kept out of sight, for the vicinity became very unhealthy for them.

The vigorous Lydia persevered in her campaign until Judge Simms was persuaded to issue the writ of *habeas corpus* requested before the trial.

"Who will go security for Lewis Wetzel's good behavior?" asked the court.

"Good behavior!" cried a woman. "Why don't you investigate before asking such a question? You must be a fool. There isn't a better mannered man in the country than Lewis Wetzel. You don't know what politeness is."

"Order in the court!" said the judge. When order was restored the question of security was again brought up. A party of hunters came forward with bags of money in their hands. "We're his bondsmen," said one.

"Have you any property?"

"Here it is," holding out the bags.

"But I mean landed property," said the court.

"Bless the man's sweet eyes," responded a naive hunter. "Just as if gold wasn't landed property. Just as if gold wasn't safer than land in these Indian settlements. Now judge, just you look here. Landed property do you say? Do you mean land? Perhaps then you'd like us to go out and dig up a whole prairie and bring it in here as security for Lewis Wetzel's decent conduct hereafter. Is that your meaning, judge?

"We don't quite get the hang of these here court proceedings, but if that's your meaning, just out with it, and if we can't lodge a whole prairie here we'll bring you the stock of one, grass, bisons, wolves and Injuns, and you can keep them all as long as you want to, judge, and bless the Injun we come across on our way out! They'll remember this day. Take the gold, judge."

"The prisoner is acquitted," said the court.

With shouts of joy Lewis Wetzel was borne on the shoulders of brawny men into the open air. Festivity reigned. The "principle" had been preserved, and in this brush with the authorities the settlers had come off best. We are told that the feasting and dancing in celebration of the famed scout's release lasted two days, during which time not an Indian showed up, nor did the smoke of a campfire cloud the sky.[85]

85. From Samuel Hildreth's *"Pioneer History of America"*; R. C. V. Myer's *"Wetzel the Scout"*, and Cecil B. Hartley's *"Life of Lewis Wetzel"*.

CHAPTER X

Return to Wheeling; Indian Hunts

FOLLOWING his acquittal Lewis accompanied Lydia to Wheeling where among friends "he could engage in his regular Indian hunting at his pleasure."

The settlers in backing Wetzel rather than the representative of law and order were not without logic. Although Wetzel's methods were not built on a grand scale or aimed at an early peace they differed from the military operations of the day in being successful, while army campaigns against the Indians were generally tragic failures.

As commander-in-chief of the United States forces General Harmar, while located at Fort Washington, led the first offensive against the Indians of western Ohio. He had some 3,000 poorly equipped soldiers, some not even having guns. In September, 1790, he led his motley array against the Indian villages on the Maumee.

The first part of his expedition was successful in that the Indians fled before he got to them, and his men then destroyed their villages without molestation, but his movements were watched by the redskins lurking in the woods. When his troops were in proper position the Reds launched an attack with such surprise and vehemence that the Whites ran in disorder.

The General ordered a counter attack, but the redskins by a ruse divided the Whites and defeated them again, in spite of heroic fighting by the Whites.

When the army got back to Fort Washington on November 3rd it had lost 183 men killed, while 37 had been wounded. In the dreary retreat it is said that the militia became so ungovernable at times that Harmar maintained

140

order only by threatening to fire on them with his artillery.

This of course did not lull the fears of the settlers, while it encouraged the Indians to go out and whoop things up some more. In fact they got so bad something had to be done, so Arthur St. Clair, then governor of the Ohio Territory, was chosen as the man to strike the blow that would take the wind out of them.

Like General Harmar, General St. Clair had good intentions but a poor army. It was underfed and ill-equipped and the 2,300 men composing it had a large assortment of inferior persons as far as soldiering is concerned. St. Clair's plan was to build a line of forts or stockades up through Ohio and thus awe the red men by the white man's powers.

St. Clair's force proceeded slowly.[86] First went scouts to spy out the land. Then came cutters to chop trees and make a road. Following them were the advance guard and then the army in two columns ending with four pieces of artillery. In the lead were horses with tents and provisions and cattle. Cavalry marched in file on the flanks and outside of the horsemen ranged riflemen and scouts. Such a cavalcade must have seemed to the watching Indians something like a circus parade. Movements of this army of course could not be kept secret.

After much hardship a fort or two were put up and then one cold morning when the men were huddled around the campfires Indians appeared in swarms and virtually exterminated them. The Americans lost 677 killed and 271 wounded, while the Indians' death toll was estimated at 150. And there were only about half as many Indians as Whites in the fray.

The Indians continued to have the best of the argument until General "Mad Anthony" Wayne thoroughly defeated them in the Battle of Fallen Timbers. Under these condi-

---

86. Jacob Wetzel was a soldier under General St. Clair. Bonnett to Draper, *Draper's Mss.*, 11E31 in the State Historical Society of Wisconsion, Madison, Wisconsin.

tions it is no wonder that a man like Wetzel who could put the fear of the white race into the frightful reds was honored by the settlers. And it is not astonishing that the settlers were not too particular about fine points when methods of warfare were considered. Wetzel fought the Indians according to their own rules, and won, while the army fought according to army rules, and lost.

When the leaves dry up and tumble down, the days grow short and mornings crisp. The deer puts on a warmer coat, while the bear and raccoon lay on fat. Wild birds leave their summer homes and wing their way to southern lands. This is the harvest time for the redman. He, too, must prepare for winter. With no grain to cut or grist to grind, no potatoes to dig or apples to pick, he hies himself away where game is thick and lays in a meat supply for the cold months.

In the old days of which this account deals the custom of hunting parties scattering to take game was still practiced by the Indians. The renewed activities of the Whites had discouraged the Reds hanging around the settlements and pilfering. They turned their steps westward in search of wild game. Deep in the shelter of the wilderness they could follow their ancient customs, probably feeling more at ease if far away from the released Lewis Wetzel, who was sojourning at the Wheeling settlement on the Ohio River.

Lewis Wetzel could not settle down. The charm and loyalty of Lydia did not break him from his roving habits. The idea of a home of his own, which would have to be kept up by manual labor, was not so entrancing as the pursuit of the most dangerous of all game—live men; while public's approval of his daring deeds could not have been lost on this laconic woodsman.

So with malice toward none—that is toward none of his recent captors, the military authorities, who "only did their duty as they understood it," he magnanimously said— Lewis bid Lydia good-bye and with his trusty rifle at hand got in a canoe and paddled away down the Ohio. The

peaceful scout idly floated down the placid river between
banks of scarlet, green and vivid yellow, nature's gayest
dress, dreamed of his innocent childhood, games with his
ragged brothers, their capture by the Indians, other attacks
by savages, then back came the smoldering fire; anew in
his mind leaped the half-forgotten oath, and the nemesis
of the redman was on the warpath once more.

Nothing of importance happened for awhile. A gentle
breeze shook down a few dying leaves, which floated lazily
away with the current. A flock of crows sheered silently
past, not anxious to arouse the strange creature with his
fearful stick that threw out fire. And on up the Muskingum
River went the traveler.

What's that? A slight movement in the bushes caught
the trained eye of the canoeman. Instinct told him that it
was time to stop. With characteristic caution he slid the
canoe under sheltering boughs and laid himself down in the
bottom of the craft to wait.

His vacation with white folks had not robbed the hunter
of his cunning, nor had the patience of a Wetzel weakened
with time. All night long he lay in the canoe. A whole
tribe of redskins might have gone through the vicinity
without discovering the thoroughly concealed and silent
White. "I scent them," said the watcher, throwing aside
all thoughts of his celebrations and life in the settlement.
He was again the primitive revengeful protector of his
race; the man with a mission, without mercy and expecting
none. The White who outdid the redman at his own game.

At the break of day he stepped ashore and hid his canoe
in the bushes. Like a panther he moved through the forest,
swift, silent, sure. The birds were not up yet, so did not
announce his approach. The shadow of a hawk flying overhead would have made as much commotion.

In the distance rose a thin thread of smoke against the
morning sky. It marked a campfire, and true as the needle
toward the pole the hunter headed for it. Down through
a glade, across a dry stream bed, over a rise of ground

glided the scout without haste but with speed. His rifle was clean and well oiled, his moccasins whole, no hanging buckskin string caught tender protruding twig, no brittle stick broke beneath the carefully placed feet, as step by step the prepared warrior advanced on his unsuspecting prey.

Worming his way through a clump of undergrowth, carefully pushing aside the tangled brush so as not to betray his presence with suddenly disturbed limbs, he neared the smoke column. Low guttural tones drifted to his sensitive ears. He crept on and presently an Indian camp appeared to his strained eyes. Pottering around it were four braves getting ready for the day's hunt.

The big, strapping fellows yawned and complained about not sleeping well, since they went to bed too early. Their ugly faces warned any attacker not to intrude without due preparation for trouble.

Leaning forward Wetzel caught from their idle conversation that they were not on the warpath, but just on a pleasure jaunt. He was on a similar errand, so could cool his heels while waiting an opportunity to present himself to the unusupecting and unguarded braves without inviting too much opposition.

At first the proposition looked a little large to the watcher. One false move and those four husky reds would conclude their pleasure jaunt by leaving a lifeless white man somewhere in the hinterlands of unexplored and unmapped Ohio. But after due consideration he decided to tackle the job, so put his mind to work on a plan of action.

Since sleeping redmen are more pleasant customers than the awake and alert article, Wetzel with his unlimited patience proceeded to wait until slumber disarmed them. The sun grew warm and the autumn odors filled the air with a sedative perfume. The melody of bird songs died; all nature dozed in the drowsy afternoon. But the vigilance of the watcher never relaxed. He saw the redmen rise, stretch and saunter off through the thicket. At this he also glided away to a more secluded spot where he could relax and rest for the coming encounter. He figured that about midnight they would be in deepest sleep.

With the setting sun the air grew chill, and Wetzel mentally placed another mark against the red race. They were making it uncomfortable for him by thus keeping him out in the cold. But he could endure hardship without flinching, so bravely bore his discomfort. The moon, a silver horn, glanced through the tree tops, then gradually withdrew under the horizon. Darkness thickened. The hour for action approached.

The scout decided to walk boldly into the camp with rifle in one hand and tomahawk in the other. If a redman awoke he could shoot him and run away through the darkness. If all slept on he could proceed to business with hand weapons. As he crept near, the dying campfire lighted a path over glistening leaves. It crackled its warning. Where is the guarding spirit of the redskin? Where is the "sixth sense" to warn the sleepers? All absent without leave.

Four blanket-covered sleeping forms lay on the ground. For a moment the white man gazed at them.

"Was he admiring their splendid physique, their calm and even breathing that told of freedom from bodily ills and a wholesome lack of fear? Was he possibly thinking of dusky women in far-off lodges dreaming of these men as no doubt Lydia Boggs was dreaming of him? Was he thinking that little children were possibly waiting for these men?"

Not Lewis Wetzel. He was thinking, but something in him was weighing chances and picking vital points on ruddy heads. He may have done some thinking while shackled in irons under military guard, but out in the open with red men before him the Wetzel method was to strike first and think afterward.

Setting his rifle against a tree with tomahawk in hand he stood over the sleepers. Down fell the weapon — one, two, three. It was all over in a jiffy. Three redskins dead and a live one running wildly through the woods. The latter had awoke at the commotion, thrown a blanket over the fire and made off before Wetzel could get him. The White chased him for some distance, but was eluded. Returning he scalped the three and headed for civilization.

"My father's life was worth far more than all of these," thought the hunter, as he hastened toward his hidden canoe.

When Lewis reached the settlement after his arduous night's work he was asked what luck he had.

"Not very good," he replied. "I found four Indians, but one got away from me. I have taken but three scalps, after all my pains and fatigue."

"Well, luck can't always go along without some disappointments," was the consoling reply of Lydia Boggs. "You must hope for better things next time."

"Oh, I don't complain. I don't complain," said the patient and stoical Lewis.

Somehow we cannot help regretting that Lydia was not a man. What a warrior she would have been.

Wetzel's defiance of military authority had got him in trouble once, but it did not teach him either respect or affection for the red brother. He had not only escaped the clutches of the law, but had emerged with honor in his own country. In all probability he did not expect that the military authorities would make a serious effort to punish him, but he knew Indians better than he did Whites and did not underestimate the effect his last raid would have on the redmen.

When the escaped warrior returned to the wigwams and told of the night attack shrill voices would demand an accounting, while grim seamy-faced braves would swear vengeance. Lewis knew he had laid a trap for himself, but feared not that he would escape it. From his ornaments one of the slain warriors was evidently a man of distinction, which further warned Wetzel of his danger.

Reports of an Indian or two in the woods were followed up by searchers, but no other trace found. The suspicious

Lewis, however, was not deceived. He felt they were on his trail, and true to his method of striking first departed on another Indian hunt. This time he was hunted as well as hunter, so called on his cunning and employed all his caution as he roamed the wilderness of Virginia.

This trip had an object other than the collection of souvenirs. It was to ferret out the intentions of the Indians toward the Whites, to learn how far the growing revolt of the redman was inciting him against the settlers, to discover if any organized attack was planned. For a time he learned nothing, except that the reds had left the neighborhood. No signs of them were seen. He began to think they had migrated West, so went on to verify this hunch, hoping to take the welcome news back to the settlements.

One night a storm came up. The wind howled over the mountains, the trees groaned and twisted, dark clouds deepened to an impenetrable black and the rain came down in bucketsful. It was a fearful night, with the lightning flashing above and the lone scout slopping along in the mud below.

Wetzel was wet to the hide and as sweet tempered as a she-bear deprived of her cubs. Seeing a ramshackle cabin ahead he edged up to it, slipped inside and groping his way climbed to the loft as the least drafty place where he might sleep. The wind howled on and the rain came down, the thunder rolled, but the man slept on. Suddenly something flashed through a consciousness so dead the elements could not enter. The thing that had awakened him was the light from the flames below, which flickering up the entrance of the loft had brought him to attention. He heard voices below.

"He come here," said one in Indian language. "He was near here all day."

"He is not here now," said another, "or he would have taken shelter here. Curse him!"

"He does not mind the weather," said the first speaker.

"Neither do we," was the answer. "But this rain is such as I never saw before."

Peeking down from his lofty shelter Lewis saw six Indians who had built a rousing fire and were preparing their supper.

"This light will attract his attention," said one of the braves.

"Good," said another. "Let it attract him. See. This hut has a loft. Let us go there and wait till he comes along. When he is thoroughly wet and tired to death, seeing the place empty he will enter."

Rather a tight squeeze, but tight places were Wetzel's pie. Drawing his knife he determined to do his best if worst came to worst. In fact he had no choice. Perhaps Daniel Boone in like predicament would have jumped down, cracked a joke or two over the Indians' heads, and run off while they were convulsed in laughter, but Wetzel was no joker. He was a serious man, and in a serious situation.

"Let's eat first," said one of the braves. "Then we'll talk about catching this slippery Lewis Wetzel." They ate ravenously, and Lewis enjoyed the meal as much as they did!

With their insides full of warm meat and their outsides drying before the warm fire the redmen grew drowsy. One of them in the midst of a long harangue, to which none listened, toppled over and slept.

"What a fool to sleep when there is so much to do," said a companion.

"What is there to do?" asked another rubbing his eyes.

"Why, is not Lewis Wetzel to be caught? Then with his scalp we will go to the white settlements, lie in wait, as he did at Fort Harmar, pick off the white cowards one by one, steal their women and children and teach them what it is to set a man free after he has murdered so many of our braves."

"Humph!" grunted the other Indians, not much impressed. They eased down into more comfortable positions.

Conversation lapsed.   Stretching out another fell asleep,
then another.

"Shall we roast Wetzel?" asked one of the three still
awake.

"We will half roast him," was the reply.

"We will then skin him perhaps?"

"We will treat him as half-roasted Crawford was treated
by Captain Pike."

The hut in the storm in which the Indians had Wetzel treed.

"Good," replied the other.   "We have much to remain
awake for."

"Good," echoed the other two.   A moment more and
one of them joined the sleepers. The remaining two humped
up before the fire, their backs toward the entrance of the
loft.

"I had a dream last night," ventured one of the reds.
"I dreamed I was in the Happy Hunting Ground, my lodge
filled with white-faced squaws, each with coal-black eyes
and cheeks red as bison's blood."

"Good," grunted the other.   "I, too, dreamed—that a

snake stung me on the heel, and it turned to a coal of fire when I tramped it. I had put my foot in the flame in my sleep."

"Ugh!" They bundled themselves up close and rocked to and fro; then ceased. They were asleep.

The watchful Wetzel gently lowered himself from the loft, his knife in his teeth ready for an emergency. An Indian stirred and the white man "froze," but the red slept on and the White gained the door and passed out into the cold and stormy night.

Tradition fails to record his thought with the painstaking detail it relates the Indians' conversation, but we may safely assume that the wet Wetzel was not thrilled with gratitude or lost in noble conceptions of kindness he would heap on the red race. He sneaked out behind a log and with his old-time patience defied the dripping elements while he awaited the coming of the dawn. After a long and wretched night during which a wolf whined piteously in his ear and slunk away in the rain, a streak of grey appeared in the East and a light appeared in the cabin.

The storm had passed. And such a storm! Trees were uprooted and the cabin looked like a wreck in a sea, surrounded as it was by the flood waters. The scout had kept his powder dry by holding it close to his body. The sun came out and smiled on a scene of desolation. It had been a bad night.

Stepping from the cabin a tall savage took in the effects of the storm, yawned, stretched his arms above his head— and the crack of a rifle came from the log hiding the scout. With smoking gun in hand Lewis Wetzel dashed away. "I could not leave them all," he remarked. Again Lewis Wetzel escaped with the characteristic flourish.[87]

---

87. From R. C. V. Myer's *"Wetzel the Scout,"* and Cecil B. Hartley's *"Life of Lewis Wetzel"*.

CHAPTER XI

BEFORE we denounce Lewis Wetzel for his apparent savagery let us remember that he was respected by his associates, and that they were in a better position to pass judgment on him than we are. His daring and success in open warfare inspired admiration, while his trial and acquittal made him a public hero. He had been willing to sacrifice himself for a principle, the principle on which the settlers based their hope of security.

Adversity thrives on persecution, and a person who is persecuted when standing for what the public thinks is right must have their admiration. We may not agree that the settlers were right in their view of the correct principle of protection, but we must confess that they had no other adequate protection than that which they took in their own hands. And we must not forget that their grievances were real, their fears well founded. The Indians which the Whites so thoroughly despised and hated were equally relentless in their opposition to the invaders, as the following event shows.

A relative of Lewis Wetzel who lived in Kentucky came to Wheeling in 1790 and invited Lewis to go home with him for a visit. Having nothing to detain him, Lewis went along. They traveled on foot, hunting as they tramped through the woods. While resting on a log one day Lewis remarked, after a period of silence, "Simon,[88] I doubt if I shall go all the way with you."

"What?" cried the young fellow. "And after all my

---

88. This was Simon Bonnett, a son of John Bonnett. See Introduction.

preparations for you? Do you know I have gathered all these birds purposely for you?"

"For me?"

"Yes. I want you to see how Tilly can cook."

"Tilly?" questioned Lewis. "Who is that?"

"Was there ever such a man!" exclaimed the boy. "Here I have been talking of Tilly, Tilly, Tilly and nothing but Tilly all the way, and you do not know who she is. Did you not know it was a young woman?"

"Old women can be named Tilly, too, I suppose," said the prosaic Lewis.

"But young men don't talk quite as much about old Tillies as I have been talking. Can't you guess who she is?"

"Maybe your sister. Maybe you told me you had a sister." Lewis pretended to be uncommonly dense.

"Maybe somebody else's sister," exploded his companion. "Upon my word, Lewis Wetzel, you are a regular Indian in your refusal to ask questions. It is not such an easy matter for a man who meets another man for the first time—and you almost a stranger to me—to tell him that he is going to be married.

"Yes, Tilly will be my wife. I wanted to surprise you when you saw her; such a beauty as she is. I suppose you know a beautiful woman when you see one?"

"Oh, I don't know," carelessly answered Lewis.

"Then you are a heathen!" replied the youth.

"Nay, Simon," said Lewis Wetzel in a softened voice. "There has been too much said about my being a heathen. I am anything rather than a heathen. I am only a weak man like other men, like you. And like other men, strong physically, my bodily excellence often makes me seem mentally deficient. People too often associate religion with weakness. Whatever my beliefs or disbeliefs may be I am never a heathen. Perhaps those with the strongest faith are not always those who speak of it."

"But you take so little interest in men and their doings," said his relative.

"I take little interest in my own doings," said the scout. "I am impelled forward to do the work of my life, and I do it. Some power within me urges me on. What it is I know not. I only know that it is the power within me.

"Now tell me about the young woman Tilly. When shall you be married? How can I help you and her? Have you a house to take her in?"

"Now that's something like it," said the other. "If there's anything I despise it is to talk on and on about the woman I love, and have people look and act as though she were just like other women. Two married women are precisely alike, as all men are alike, but a young woman in love for the first time is unlike anything on earth, although there may be millions of young women who are in the same pickle with herself. The pickle is the same; the young women are not. Do you see?"

"I fail to see," said Lewis. "It is not your fault, Simon. And maybe I appreciate pickles better than I do women. Yet a woman is something sacred."

The younger man was gay as they proceeded, each weary mile lightened by thoughts which ran before. No longer did the travelers loiter in search of game, but hastened on with best speed toward the new cabin Simon Bonnett had built for his expectant bride.[89] He pictured the meeting when they should reach her home, the little house in the clearing, now partially vine covered and with flowers springing up to show their appreciation of her thoughtful care. Perhaps the girl herself would be standing in the doorway.

With quickened steps the youth led the way over familiar ground, Lewis Wetzel following with his eyes on the

89.   Some historians say the cabin stood on Crow's Creek, Marshall County, West Virginia, and the trail was followed to Captina, Marshall County, where the Indians and captive crossed the river. However, this seems incorrect from the best historians of to-day and the above version seems to be the true account of the rescue of Tilly and the rescue of Rose Forester by Lewis Wetzel and Albert Maywood at another time was the Crow Creek affair.

trail. "Only a short distance," cried the lover as he broke from the woods into the open space. Wetzel did not raise his eyes until a shriek brought him to attention. Where was the pretty picture of a vine-clad cottage and a brown-eyed girl. Where ——? Before them lay a pile of smoking ruins.

When the extent of the tragedy dawned upon him Simon fell to the ground. Wetzel was also on his hands and knees, not from shock but to examine the trail that had drawn his attention as they came toward the clearing. He arose, shook the prostrate youth to his feet and said sternly, "Be a man!"

"A man?" said Simon Bonnett. "I will be a devil!"

"Don't be too harsh in your threats," advised Lewis. "It may not be as bad as you think. There have not been Indians here alone. This trail proves that three Indians and one white man took away the captive."

"Then there is a little hope," ventured the lad.

"Not from the white man," said Wetzel. "Come. We will go. There is nothing to keep us here."

"Nothing," groaned the young man. "And yet it was everything."

With Wetzel now in the lead the two struck the abductors' trail, hoping to catch them before they crossed the Ohio. The still smoking ruin showed that the attack had been made that day.

Presently the fresh trail disappeared. The foxy captors had covered it to hide their flight.

"That is the cursed spite of the red devils," cried the heart-broken youth.

"Rather it is the work of the white man," said the cool and calculating Lewis. "I have a plan. Follow me and keep up a brave hope." He spoke more hopefully than he felt, perhaps, but did it to give his companion strength and courage. They left the trail and cut across the country to intercept the redskins where he figured they would cross the river.

"Oh, my dear could never go so far," said Simon.

"She could if she were forced to," replied Lewis.

"Who would dare force her?" said the other.

"That is right," said Lewis. "Only keep up that spirit and you may be of some service to the woman you think and almost constantly say you love." Rough words, but they had the desired effect.

"The woman I say I love?" repeated the boy.

"Yes. I have only your word for it," quoth the phlegmatic Lewis. "You have not demonstrated the fact."

Without waiting a reply he pushed on. In an hour they struck a deer path which topped the knolls and thus saved time through the curves of ravines. The men were taking the shortest distance to the point at which they were aiming.

Night fell and the moon came out. No stop for supper. Simon was so busy with thoughts of other moon-lit nights that he forgot to eat until Lewis fished some food from his pocket and said, "Eat this."

"Eat at such a time as this!" cried the lover.

"Then don't do it, and you will have no strength to rescue the woman you love," said his practical companion. The boy took the food and ate it.

They kept going until about midnight, when clouds came up and hid the path.

"We shall have to rest until morning," said Lewis.

"Oh, my dear; my dear! Will it ever be morning again for you and me?" sobbed his friend.

In silence and misery they lived through the long, dark hours until dawn at last appeared. On glancing at his friend, Lewis noted a change in the boy; there was a new look of determination in his face, a dignity in his bearing, a promise in his eyes.

Falling on his knees the young man prayed, while Lewis bowed his head. "I have seldom prayed," said the youth as he calmly rose. "But my dear told me she always prayed when she was in any difficulty or danger. Wherever she was last night, she was thinking of me and praying for me.

Wherever she is at this moment her eyes are raised above and she is asking divine guidance and support.

"I prayed all last night that I might be in communion with her, that my words might meet hers in their flight to heaven and be assisted by hers to reach the throne of mercy. Now let us go on."

With head still bowed Lewis Wetzel pressed his friend's hand and the two resumed the chase.

Down from the ridge on which they had traveled they came to a deep and quiet valley, a wild place untouched by hand of man, red or white. Here in the soft soil they spied fresh foot prints. And joy of joys! the mark of a little shoe with nail heads around the heel. The trail was plain and the hunters followed it with the speed and assurance of bloodhounds. Hour after hour the little shoe with nail heads in the midst of moccasin tracks led them on. Over hills, through valleys—the pursued lost no time, and the pursuers called on all their strength to reach the river first. Vain hope. Through the trees the placid Ohio shimmered in the late afternoon sun, but the captors were still ahead.

What is that on the opposite shore? Sure enough, a camp! The kidnappers had stopped to rest after crossing the river, just below the mouth of the Muskingum.

"Can you swim?" asked Wetzel. But his companion was already in the water. Together they swam the stream and climbed the bank out of the sight of the enemy's camp.

"We'll wait until morning and then get the girl away from the red rascals," said the cool and patient Lewis.

"Wait!" cried the other. "What can the words mean to her in the hands of those red devils?"

"I don't fear for her safety with the red cusses as much as I do with the white man," said the wise scout. "A white man on friendly terms with these marauding Indians is worse than a devil. He is a depraved saint."

"But I cannot wait until day," said his friend.

"You must," ordered Lewis. "You have got to be as wary as your enemy. Make an attempt to-night and the chances are that the first load you fire will disperse the red-skins, and you will find your lady love—"

"Yes?"

"A corpse. If the Indians did not murder her the white man with them would."

The youth saw the point of this argument and the two settled down for a night of Wetzel waiting. No sleep for the watchers; they were as silent as the trees which sheltered them, but as alert as the owl that perched like a statue overhead listening to faintest sound that would betray the location of a meal.

With the coming of the dawn the savages were astir making ready to continue their journey.

"Take good aim at the white man," whispered Lewis. "He is your worst enemy. I will look out for my beloved Indians."

Already the anxious youth was pointing his gun.

"Careful," cautioned Lewis. "Don't for the life of you miss him. For your lady love let your shot be. Now!" Two shots rang out, each true to its mark.

Throwing down his gun the youth rushed forward to be met by his frightened sweetheart, as the two remaining Indians took to their heels through the timber.

Lewis stepped aside until the tableau was ended, then approached the young folks. Throwing out his arm in the direction of a white settlement, which lay within half a mile of the scene of rescue, he said, "That is your way back. Go seek it."

"But Lewis, come here," was the reply.

"My way lies in another direction. Farewell," said the scout. He moved into the woods after the two fleeing Indians.

They were not to be seen, so he fired his rifle in hope of drawing them from their hiding places. The ruse succeeded. Believing him handicapped with an empty gun the reds dashed at their pursuer. Here they erred in judgment.

Sprinting away the versatile scout reloaded on the run, whirled and shot the nearest red.

The other red came on with uplifted tomahawk, but Lewis Wetzel dodged from tree to tree and kept out of reach until he had a chance to load once more. Turning he finished this Indian as he had the others, methodically scalped all of them, and trudged toward the settlement in time to see the reunited lovers, arm in arm, entering the shelter of civilization.

The man of destiny, who took little interest in the private affairs of his friends, or even in himself, but who felt impelled by some hidden power to carry out his mission of protecting his race, gazed long at the departing figures. Sure of himself, fanatically faithful in his self-imposed trust, could he doubt the wisdom of his choice or the existence of the force that sent him to combat fellow beings; or did he sense something lacking in his life, which was so apparent in the departing figures? Which was the wiser man, the happy youth or the grave scout?

The untutored mind of the ranger gave up the puzzling problem as he unconsciously slung his rifle in the hollow of his arm and turned away from the settlement. Whatever lure civilization held for him, there was always something stronger in the call of the wild. Like beckoned to like as Wetzel chose the uncharted trail.

He was not alone in this kindred feeling for the untamed woods. Scores of others turned their backs on civilization during these years and cast their lots with the Indians. In most cases these were captives, who after the first shock of separation had worn off found the care-free life of the redmen preferable, as far as they were concerned, to the more restricted and regulated existence of the Whites. In many instances white captives, when released by their captors or exchanged as a part of some treaty or peace settlement, refused to leave the redmen's tepees for the white men's houses. This, of course, was not universal as many were glad to return to their friends and families after years of captivity, but it did happen. At one time when white prisoners were brought to Pittsburgh and released by Indians, they had to be restrained forcibly by the Whites to make them stay "tamed," even going so far as to break away and run back to the woods again. Wetzel differed from these lovers of the wild life in that he never severed his connections with the Whites or relented in any measure of his distrust and dislike of the reds. However little use he may have appeared to have for civilization he has the distinction of unswerving loyalty to his race, singleness of his purpose and thoroughness of his craft.[90]

Lewis Wetzel and Albert Maywood Rescued Rose Forester From the Indians

There lived in Virginia before the Revolutionary War two wealthy planters, named Maywood and Forester. They had been intimate in their youth, and had grown up friends in the true sense of the term. They had married at nearly the same period, and settled down side by side, each having a fortune sufficient to give him an easy independence.

At the outbreak of the Revolutionary War, Maywood had two sons of the ages of seven and four, and Forester one daughter of three years. Both were patriotic men and, feeling that their country needed them, both volunteered their services in her defense. Forester received the rank of Colonel, and Maywood that of Captain from the government, in commissions granted them. The government being embarrassed for funds to pay the soldiers or even supply them with the necessary clothing and provisions, these two noble patriots mortgaged their plantations and put the amount received from them into a quartermaster's hands, to be used for the benefit of the regiment. At the Battle of Cowpens that was fought in 1781, Colonel Forester fell mortally wounded. Captain Maywood was near when he was shot from his horse, and raised him in his arms and bore him through a terrible fire to the quarters of the sur-

90. From R. C. V. Myer's *"Wetzel the Scout."*

geon who, on examining his wounds, shook his head and said that Forester did not have many minutes to live. On hearing this the dying soldier, who had received word of his wife's death a month before, was composed, and remarked that such was the fate of war. "In a few minutes," he said, "I shall be with my angel wife in another world, and there will be none but you, my friend, to act the part of father to my sweet child, Rose Forester. In your care I leave her. Farewell, my friend, and may God preserve you to behold the day when the Stars and Stripes shall wave in triumph over a land of free men."

These were the last words of Colonel Forester. In less than five minutes he was a corpse, and his friend stood beside him weeping at the loss of a bosom companion and comrade.

At the close of the war Captain Maywood returned to his family, of which "little Rose Forester" was already a member. In 1789 Captain Maywood removed with his family to Dunkard Creek, which was a branch of Wheeling Creek but at present is known as Crow's Creek and the south forth of Wheeling Creek, in Marshall county, Webster district, near Majorsville, West Virginia. He erected a cabin on a knoll. There were few settlers in this section of the country, but little trouble was expected from the Indians so the bold pioneers took no pains to guard against their attacks.

His eldest son, Albert Maywood, an intelligent youth of 20, tried to warn his father of the dangers from an Indian attack, on the grounds that the Indians had long been at war with the Whites; but all his warnings were taken as gestures or imaginations and made his father more obstinate than ever.

Two things seemed to absorb Albert Maywood's whole thoughts. They were his rifle and Rose Forester. To range the woods all day with his rifle and return at night to sit and talk with Rose was to him the acme of delight and the soul of his enjoyment.

One day in the fall of 1791, he was hunting on the waters of Wheeling Creek when he met his friend, Lewis Wetzel. He invited Wetzel to go home with him and visit the family, which invitation he accepted. They started up the creek toward the Maywood home hunting; they traveled slowly along not thinking of any need to hurry or any dangers to the home at the end of their journey. When they arrived at the home of Maywood they found that the Indians had been there, murdered the family and burned the house and barn. Wetzel examined the trail and found that the party consisted of three Indians, a white man, and that five had left the log cabin and from the tracks it was decided that Rose Forester was a prisoner in the hands of the Indians and the white renegade. The rest of the family, including Captain Maywood, his wife, son, and daughter were all murdered and burned within the cabin. Wetzel and Albert, after viewing the smoking remains of the house and barn, dug a large grave and buried all the bodies in it side by side. Wetzel's courage inspired Albert and gave him strength to follow him and they took up the trail of the marauders and headed for the Ohio River as fast as they could travel. It was late in the day and the Indians had a considerable start on them. Caution had been taken to conceal their trail but the quick eye of Wetzel soon detected it.

Wetzel and Maywood followed the trail like bloodhounds until Wetzel was satisfied at about the point they would reach the river. He then changed his plan and took the most direct route to the Ohio river at the point at which he was sure they would reach to cross. This was at the mouth of Big Captina Creek. The knowledge that Wetzel had of the country enabled them to save distance and the desire to avenge the murder of the Maywood family animated them; and as Albert was very anxious to rescue Rose Forester they kept on at full speed until they crossed a stream and on the margin of it they detected the impression of a heel of a shoe that was identical with the one of the

woman they found at the cabin, and which had left with
the three Indians and a White man. The freshness of the
track was enough to satisfy Wetzel that they were gaining
on them. Late in the evening they reached the Ohio River
at Hog Run, in Franklin district, Marshall County, W. Va.,
nearly opposite the mouth of Big Captina Creek, and found
that the murderers with their captive had reached the river
first and were now on the Ohio side of it. Wetzel was not
the least discouraged but confident of overtaking them and
rescuing the girl. They went down the river a short distance and swam it. By the time Wetzel and Maywood were
ready to start in pursuit of the murderers on the west side
of the river, darkness had settled down over the forest but
they were ready for a night's travel. They found the Indians and captive encamped a short distance from the river.

The Indians and White renegade were lying near the
fire and Rose Forester was securely bound and tied to a
small tree. She was moaning and bewailing her misfortune
not thinking that friends were close at hand. Maywood
was in favor of attacking the camp at once but Wetzel
would not listen to it and persuaded him to wait until daylight.

The first streaks of gray dawn in the East found Wetzel
and Maywood ready for action. The Indians and white
man, whom they recognized to be Jim Girty, arose and were
standing about the fire when the stillness of the morning
was broken by the report of two rifles, Jim Girty and one
of the Indians fell dead. Wetzel had killed the Indian and
Maywood had killed Jim Girty; as Lewis Wetzel had always
said that his hands were never red by the blood of a white
man or woman; be she red or white; but he had sworn
vengeance against the males of the Indian race.. The other
two Indians ran into the forest closely followed by Wetzel.
He failed to draw their fire and he fired his gun at random
to get them after him. They dropped their guns and with
their tomahawks waving above their heads took after the
hunter. That was their last race. Wetzel's gun was soon

loaded and the foremost Indian was shot dead; but the other one continued the race for the long black scalp; soon the mysterious gun was again loaded and the last Indian was shot through the heart. Maywood sprang to Rose Forester and cut the cords binding her, as soon as the first two shots were fired, leaving Wetzel to cope with the two remaining Indians alone. Returning with the three Indian scalps, Wetzel told Albert and Rose to remain there until he returned as he disappeared into the forest in search of game.

A deer came bounding by and thinking that Wetzel was frightening it toward them, Albert shot it. It was soon skinned and morsels of it were being broiled over a fire. Albert and Rose both agreed that it was the best deer meat that they had ever eaten.

Albert returned to the deer to secure some more meat to have ready for Wetzel when he returned; when suddenly he heard a shriek from Rose. Hardly conscious of what he did, he sprang for his rifle but it was too late. Already a swarthy savage had grasped it, and the horrid yells of twenty more had sounded in his ear. At the same moment a blow on the head from behind laid him senseless upon the earth.

When Albert again recovered his senses he found himself lying on his back with several savages standing around him holding a consultation; but not where he had fallen. When Albert had risen the Indian said, in broken English, "Me, Ogwehea, great warrior kill to scalp," holding up eight fingers to indicate he had scalped eight Whites. "Tarhe, great chief," pointing to him. "Paleface brave; him kill so warriors," holding up four fingers to denote the number slain.

"Ogwehea, tell me whether the girl is living or dead?" Albert asked.

"Squaw dead," answered Ogwehea.

Albert did not know what to tell the Indians next, about the four missing scalps that Lewis Wetzel had in his possession, for fear they would kill or capture Wetzel if they knew he was near.

The Indians started for their village with Albert Maywood. The party divided and, thinking that Rose was dead and that he would be burned at the stake or otherwise tortured to death, before Wetzel could rescue him, and his wound on the head all made him wish the Indians would tomahawk him at once.

They followed the bed of a stream for several miles toward the Ohio River. Ogwehea commanded the party when finally they selected a place on a knoll to encamp for the night. Albert was tied, hand and foot to a small tree, by a strip of deerskin passed around his neck, arms, and ankles. His captors offered him food and water of which he partook freely. Before the Indians retired for the night they placed him on his back and bound his wrists to a stick that ran between his shoulders. Thus he passed the night in agony. When daylight came they loosened him and continued on their journey into Ohio. The second night they encamped on the northern bank of the Muskingum. None of the Indian scouts that had been sent out that day had returned when they settled down for the night, and this gave the Indians some uneasiness. Towards morning a heavy rain quenched the fire and saturated the deer thongs that bound him; which gave him some comfort.

In the darkness and rain he heard, "the song of the whippoorwill." It ceased, the rain had stopped and the Indians were deep in slumber. After a lapse of fifteen or twenty minutes after hearing, "the song of the whippoorwill," during which Albert had heard nothing but the deep roar of the forest and a pack of howling wolves in the distance; he felt something cold touch one of his outstretched hands. On turning his eyes in that direction he beheld the glittering blade of a knife attached to a long stick, one end of which was concealed behind a large sycamore tree. Slowly the knife turned, guided by an unseen hand, and gliding under his wrists it severed the thongs that bound his arm. This was carefully moved to the other, and the ligament cut in the same manner. Albert now felt that he was free. Raising himself carefully, he cautiously moved toward the large sycamore tree where the mysterious agent was concealed. Lewis Wetzel placed his hand on Albert's shoulder and whispered to get a rifle and "let's be going". Albert secured a rifle and started again for freedom. He had only gone a few steps when he pressed on a dry stick. It snapped with a loud noise and instantly one of the savages sprang up and gave a yell that awakened the others. At the same moment Albert sprang behind the tree; the crack of Lewis Wetzel's rifle was heard and the savage bounding from the earth, with a yell, fell dead. The others suddenly aroused from their sleep stood for an instant bewildered. That moment was fatal to another, for the report of Albert's rifle rang out, and another was dead in his tracks. With yells of dismay the other two Indians bounded into the hazel thicket fleeing as fast as their legs would carry them.

About twelve months after this when Lewis Wetzel and Albert Maywood were hunting they discovered a large Indian village above the mouth of the Hockhocking River on the northern bank of the Ohio, now near Belpre, Ohio. They reached a steep precipice, called "Standing Stone," where they could overlook a large Wyandotte and Huron village of over one hundred wigwams. The scouts found a place in the rocks near the top of the hill where they could live comfortably for a long time if necessary, fortified on all sides by nature. The scouts, with the aid of a spyglass, could watch the fall games of the savages without being detected. They could see Ogwehea and Tarhe in plain view, and the scouts' blood boiled because they were the ones that had captured Albert Maywood and said that they had killed Rose Forester.

The scouts had lived in the rock cave on the top of the hill for two days when their water supply was gone and Albert started out in search of a spring. Keeping in the thicket of hazel brush he moved along the banks of the

Hockhocking until he found a fine spring of water. Filling his canteen and slinging it over his shoulder he started back when he heard light steps behind him. Grasping his rifle and turning about he suddenly beheld two squaws within a few feet of him. He perceived that one was young and the other old. The old one uttered a low peculiar whoop and the young one gave a sharp startled scream. It was a fearful moment because another scream would bring upon him a whole band of warriors and certain death. He quickly resolved that both must die, and that the noise of the rifle would be fatal to himself, therefore the death must be noiseless. The Hockhocking was flowing nearby; its waters breast high. Albert dropped his rifle and bounded forward, seized the squaws by the throat and dragged them into the swift waters all in a minute's time. In a moment both were submerged; but instantly the younger raised her head above the water and when she could speak called "Albert". Now thinking that the old squaw was the most to be feared he kept her head under the water until "the old hag" sank to the bottom. He then swam to the side of the younger who was struggling alone and he gasped, "It is Rose Forester". Grasping her in his arms he carried her safely to the shore. She accompanied Albert to the home in the rocks on the top of the hill. Both Wetzel and Albert tried to persuade her to go back to the Indian village, where she had lived for over a year and had been adopted as a squaw, and return to them in the woods later. Rose would not listen to them but said she was going to help them fight it out. The Indians missing the two squaws gave the war-whoop and started on their trail up the steep hill. The first redskin that came within rifle shot was met by a bullet from "Old kill nigger", which was Lewis Wetzel's rifle. As the Indian rolled down the steep hill Wetzel remarked, "That is his last sickness". The battle was on between Lewis Wetzel and Albert Maywood and 500 Wyandotte and Huron Indians.

Rose disappeared and Wetzel and Maywood kept picking the Indians off as they came up the steep hill, but they came so fast during the battle that one Indian crept to a rock and was about to tomahawk Wetzel and Maywood before they could get their guns reloaded. A mysterious shot rang out from the bushes at the side and the redskin rolled down the steep embankment. This happened three times during the day and night that the battle raged. Among the Indians that fell was Ogwehea. The Indians finally gave up and returned to the village. The mysterious marksman proved to be Rose Forester. When the first Indian fell, Rose ran and secured his rifle, and powder and shot pouch before the other Indians could get to her. She hid herself in the bushes at the side to aid the scouts. She had learned to shoot well since living among the Indians. She beckoned the scouts to follow her as she led them through the center of the Indian village while the savages were in deep slumber. They traveled all night and the next day; as they did not stop to rest until danger was at least partly over.

The Indians were not able to overtake them and three days later they arrived at Fort Harmar. The governor tendered both Lewis Wetzel and Albert Maywood a commission in the territorial militia for their services to their country. Wetzel refused but Maywood accepted; therefore Albert Maywood bore the rank of Captain, which was the same title as his father bore in the Revolutionary War.

A few days after the arrival of Captain Albert Maywood and Rose Forester at Camp Martius they were married by the governor himself, officiating as magistrate in the presence of the whole garrison.

Lewis Wetzel seeing his friend, Albert Maywood, united to the being of his choice, and knowing he would hunt Indians no more with him; took a tearful leave of each and again returned to the forest in his accustomed vocation of Indian hunter, scout and spy.

Albert and Rose never saw Lewis Wetzel again, but they heard of his gallant deeds on the Northwestern frontier, and subsequently that he had departed to the still further far West beyond the bounds of approaching civilization.[91]

A young man by the name of Reynolds came from east of the mountains to Wheeling to await an opportunity of going down in Kentucky. This was in 1786 or 1787. There was a young woman living in Wheeling, named Rose Kennedy. Reynolds being a handsome young man began paying his attentions to Rose Kennedy. They soon became engaged and agreed that they should first get her parents' consent. One morning Rose and Reynolds were ready to start on horseback to her parents' home, on Buffalo Creek, some sixteen or eighteen miles from Wheeling, to secure their consent to marry. As they were ready to ride off, each one riding a horse, Lewis Wetzel just returned from a hunting trip and cautioned the lovers to take their guns with them, and not to follow the river road but to take the road across the hill. Fearing the young folks would not obey, he warned them the second time. However, they did not take Wetzel's advice but took the road along the river. They had gone but four or five miles when a fine large buck deer with two smaller deer stood gazing at the two lovers as they rode up. Reynolds could not resist the temptation but alighted from his horse and shot the large one. He fell but finally got up and started through the dense forest with Reynolds after it, leaving Rose in charge of the horses. She had also dismounted and seated herself on a log holding the two bridles while Reynolds pursued the deer. He followed it a few hundred yards when it turned and came back on the same trail. He no sooner came in sight of Rose and the horses than he spied four Indians. Two of them in the act of tying Rose's delicate hands together with a cord, while the other two had taken charge of the horses, and were watching in the direction of Reynolds. The shot had been heard by the

91. *Forest Rose*, by Emerson Bennett, Outcalt and Co., Lancaster, Ohio, 1861.

Indians and they came skulking up to investigate its cause. One could speak English and Rose told him that Reynolds had shot a deer and was in pursuit of it.

Reynolds made his way back to the fort at Wheeling with all possible speed and told what had happened. Eight or ten men were ready to start in a few minutes but Lewis Wetzel's advice must be first sought on this matter. Wetzel said, "I will go and bring Rose Kennedy and the horses back safe, but not more than one can accompany me". It was soon agreed that Reynolds should go with Wetzel, as he insisted on going and there was no time to parley. Wetzel cautioned Reynolds to obey his instructions. They started with Wetzel in the lead along the river road; when they came to the mouth of Short Creek, Wetzel began to watch the river. He told Reynolds to keep a profound silence, a steady nerve and a cool head. Wetzel began to investigate the sandbar, the thick willow thicket, and a large pile of driftwood. He noticed the willow bushes had been cut and bent down. Upon examining it carefully, he found their canoes hidden there. Lewis whispered to Reynolds that they would soon have "some sport." Hiding themselves in a selected place by the driftwood pile, and priming their guns carefully they were ready for any emergency. They did not have long to wait. Presently, Wetzel spied two Indians creeping down the bank looking intently in the direction of their canoe. One was a very large, robust fellow, and the other one was a small Indian. The large one was leading Rose Forester by a cord fastened to her arm, and her hands were tied. They proceeded toward their canoe. When opposite Wetzel and Reynolds they made a halt, and the big Indian was telling the little Indian to go bring the canoe round the driftwood pile, so that they might get in. Wetzel thought that was the proper time. The lovely, charming girl was standing between the two Indians. Lewis signalled to Reynolds to take a dead aim at the little Indian and kick him with his foot when he was ready to shoot. Both took deliberate aim; two shots rang out and the two

Indians fell dead. Wetzel had enough to do to keep them from speaking aloud. Knowing that there were two more Indians near, he told Reynolds to recharge his gun and conceal himself behind the log again where he had been, and to remain there until he returned. He took Rose and hid her in a pawpaw thicket, with orders to remain there until

(Courtesy of Miss Beeda McWhorter)

Dr. Weidman of Martins Ferry, Ohio, owns this Indian Paint Bag which Lewis Wetzel captured from the Indians on this occasion. The Indian Paint Bag was used by the Indians to carry their war paint in, which was a mixture of various kinds of clay. They said the white man did not know where to find war paint.

he came for her. Rose apparently did not think that Wetzel
was in any danger with the other two Indians. Reynolds
did not know where Wetzel had placed Rose but he waited
patiently and nervously for Wetzel and Rose's return. Of
course, both Rose and Reynolds heard every faint noise,
and every chirp of a bird. After a while they heard the report of Wetzel's trusty rifle through the profound silence and
in a short time the second report was heard; then the snort-
ing of the horses and the trampling of their hoofs were
heard coming down the river path. Rose peeped from her
hiding place and could see Lewis Wetzel leading both horses
and he told her to come and get on her horse. "Imagine her
thrill at this time, also that of her lover." Wetzel went up
the river a short distance to where there is a bend. Striking the Indians' trail there and following it a few hundred
yards, he hid himself carefully and waited. In a few minutes he spied one Indian holding the two horses. He
crawled cautiously along until he came opposite the Indian
and the horses. He shot that one dead in his tracks as he
was holding the horses at arm's length. The horses being
frightened and loose began to trot down the river path.
Wetzel soon had his gun reloaded and ready for action
again. He waited where he was. The fourth Indian apparently had gone down the river to ascertain if the others
had crossed in the canoe safely. He heard the shot up the
river and had started back up to investigate, and seeing the
two horses coming down he caught them by the bridle and
came on up the river path.

Wetzel in the meantime had slipped down the bank a
little ways and hid himself behind a tree. When the Indian
and the horses appeared close enough, Wetzel with a deadly
aim put an end to the fourth Indian. Scalping the Indians
and taking the two horses, also Rose Kennedy and Reynolds
started back to Wheeling. They were all safe in the fort before sundown with the satisfaction of an afternoon's work.

The big Indian proved to be Canipsico, the great Mingo

chief, who had committed many murders among the Whites.[92-93]

---

92.   Neither Peter Spicer nor any other White renegade was in this episode.   Peter Spicer lived for many years after this.
93.   Lewis Bonnett to Lyman C. Draper.   *Draper's Mss.*, 11E28 and 11E29 in the State Historical Society of Wisconsin, Madison, Wisconsin.

CHAPTER XII

First Trip to the Southwest

B ACK in Wheeling again the wanderlust proved stronger than love for home, peace or security. Even the charms of Lydia Boggs failed to hold him when the notion struck him that he should explore new territory. He had in mind a trip to the Southwest and to this end secured passage on a flatboat for New Orleans. The faithful Lydia saw him off and as the boat moved down the Ohio the scout sat on deck, silent and a little sad.

No record remains of this trip, how the travelers ate, slept or passed the hundreds of miles of Indian-infested and tree-clad shores to the Father of Waters and on down toward the old French settlement. We are told, however, that he preserved his poise of indifference, answering when spoken to but starting no conversation of his own accord. A sick man on board aroused his interest. This man had given up hope and was going home to die.

To the tragic mind of Wetzel this was something worth while and he listened with sympathetic interest to the sick man's account of his life and his longing to see his "sunny South and heaven" again. Wavering between this and the next world the invalid dwelt on his conception of the future.

"There is no more disappointment in Heaven," said he. "Those we love love us. Do you believe in this?"

"I believe. Oh, yes," replied Lewis.

"My Heaven is in the South, the glorious South," said the homesick man.

True to his self-imposed task as protector Wetzel did not leave his companion when they reached New Orleans. "Have you any friends?" he asked his charge.

"Friends?" echoed the other, smiling. "Friends! Many, many."

"They are not here to receive you," said Wetzel.

"They did not expect me so soon," he was told. "My friends will be here soon. Don't you stay here with me. Go to your own friends."

"They are not in New Orleans," said Lewis.

"Where are they?"

"I do not know."

The sick man grasped the scout's hand and said, "It will be all right some day."

"It is all right now," said Wetzel. He stayed with the ill traveler until the latter's people came and claimed him. This charitable act performed Lewis again turned his back on civilization. He did not tarry in the city, but with rifle at hand struck out through unknown wilderness.

Months passed without word from him. Even if he had been living in town he could not have written to his friends in the North, for he had never learned to read or write. This oversight in his education got him in trouble. During his sojourn in the wilds of the South he took some furs, which he sold to a dealer who had more greed than honesty in his make-up. This scoundrel paid the illiterate Wetzel for the furs with a counterfeit bill. Lewis, not being able to read, knew the amount only by the figures on the bill, and not suspecting anything wrong with it, passed it on to another. The fraud was discovered and traced back to Wetzel. The dealer having disappeared, Lewis was left to bear the blame, which was two years in prison for counterfeiting.

There seems no doubt but that Wetzel was the victim of circumstances in this case, for he had no particular use for money and there is nothing in his other acts to indicate that he would be tempted to counterfeit, or that he possessed the cleverness to do it.

He served his term in prison and at the end of two years was let out, not a hardened criminal soured against the world, but still the lone defender of the weak or the needy. Like a true knight errant of old he rushed to the rescue when he saw a ruffian insulting a girl on the street, rapping the fellow over the head with his rifle butt as a reminder to be good. He thrashed a man for using profanity toward a woman. Although we do not know the extent or nature of the provocation, we shall assume on general principles that Lewis was in the right. At least his intentions were beyond criticism. This was also the case when he found lost children and took the trouble to restore them to their parents.

Wetzel lived apart and alone, even in the midst of men; while he showed slight concern about their affairs they were less indifferent to his. One day on the street a stranger hailed him as "Captain".

"I'm not a captain,'' said Lewis sharply. "I'm Lewis Wetzel."

"How are bears up your way?" asked the stranger.

"How do you know me?" asked Lewis.

"Why, your name is all through New Orleans," said the other. "Everybody has heard of Lewis Wetzel." And why not? His garb and adherence to his rifle even in town were enough to single him out to the curious minded.

Lewis was master of his fate in the untamed woods. Neither strange wilderness nor hostile redskins held any terror for him. He was at home here where others would have died of fright or starvation, but he did not get along so well in haunts of men as he did in the haunts of Indians and wild animals. Some time after he got out of jail he got in again.

"He boarded with a Spaniard who lived a mile out of town. The Spaniard had moulds to run dollars, and one day while he was in New Orleans, Wetzel ran some pewter dollars for the children to play with. Some time after this, the Spaniard became jealous of Wetzel and made oath that Lewis Wetzel coined the pewter dollars; he also accused him of an intrigue with a Spanish girl, of which he was later found to be as innocent as he was of counterfeiting. At the trial the Spaniard used the pewter dollars as evidence against Wetzel and he was confined to prison. The Spaniard was also convicted of counterfeiting and was placed in a cell adjoining that of Wetzel's. There was a small hole in the partition and Wetzel called the Spaniard to come there as he wanted to talk to him. When the Spaniard came Wetzel put his arm through the opening and tried to kill him with a dirk that he had secured in some unknown manner. He failed in the attempt but this cost him eighteen months in irons in one of the cells.

"After Wetzel spent five years and some months in prison, John Miner, from New Brownsville, Pa., went to New Orleans as a trader. He learned of Wetzel being in prison, and as he was well acquainted with him, he began to plan for his release. Miner finally succeeded in bribing the governor and the keeper of the prison. Wetzel said that he was sick and about dead. Miner procured a coffin and conveyed it to his cell. Lewis was supposed to have died and he was put into the coffin and taken to the burying ground. The burying ground was no sooner reached than Lewis Wetzel burst out and ran for a vessel that was ready to set sail for New York. The governor wrote to the King of Spain that such a prisoner was dead, and that was the last of the case; as the empty coffin was buried. This incarceration seems to have been enough of the 'sunny South' for him, as he hurried home as soon as the boat landed in New York, going by way of Philadelphia.

"In the City of Brotherly Love our hero went to church on Sunday. Among the congregation that day was one George Washington, then President of the United States. We are told that while in Philadelphia Wetzel was greeted by Washington, but what passed between those two, history fails to record. Possibly Lewis reported on bear hunting conditions in Louisiana, or maybe the dignified President and the taciturn scout found something in common in comparing notes on other conditions in the edge of the new country.

"From Philadelphia Wetzel journeyed to Wheeling where the faithful Lydia Boggs awaited him. He told Lydia that he would never be satisfied until he repaid the Spaniard who had wronged him."[94]

---

94. Lewis Bonnett told Lyman C. Draper that Lewis Wetzel told him this with his own mouth. Extract from a letter of Nov. 8, 1846, Lewis Bonnett to Lyman C. Draper. *Draper's Mss.*, 11E87, of the State Historical Society of Wisconsin, Madison, Wisconsin.

CHAPTER XIII

The Changed and New Lewis Wetzel

S HE MUST have noted a change in his manner, for time and experience were leaving their marks. For one thing he was kinder toward his mother, and for two days visited her at Wheeling Creek at Jacob Wetzel's, his younger brother.

Lewis could never forgive the man for wanting to marry her; at any rate he was too stubborn to pretend to forgive, but he listened with patience to her praises of the man, now a prosperous herder.[95]

"You are more like you were when you were very young, Lewis," said the glad mother. "Ah, I remember the time I sat in the bottom of the wagon and watched our little home disappearing."

"Well, what are you crying about?" said her son not unkindly. "That's all over years ago."

"Cry! Why, I have always cried about you. I cried that day in the wagon till you were all damp. Cry! Women have always cried about you. When we heard that you were arrested in New Orleans . . . ."

"Who cried, for instance, but you mother?"

"Why, Lydia Boggs cried, almost her eyes out and said she just knew you were not guilty of any crime," said the mother.

"I mean to avenge those arrests," remarked Lewis quietly.

---

95. Mary Bonnett, Wetzel's sweetheart, died suddenly a few days before the marriage was to take place. She never married a second time and lived with her son, Jacob Wetzel, who bought out the other heirs at the death of his father, Captain John Wetzel. Bonnett to Draper, *Drapers Mss.*, 24S47 in the State Historical Society of Wisconsin, Madison, Wisconsin.

His mother then told him the story of Lizzie Pheister and the flag, ending with, "There was a fine figure of a woman, none of your western breed there."

"There is nothing against the western women, mother," said Lewis.

This gave the old lady an opening for a subject she had been wanting to broach. "Lewis," said she, "you are get-

Log cabin in Marshall County occupied by Lewis Wetzel about 1795.

ting old. It is time you should be thinking of settling down like the rest of us. I know the sweetest, smartest, gentlest creature in the world, and she thinks you are the boldest, brazenest, hatefulest, fearfulest man in creation; and that is next to saying that she is head over ears in love with you." From which statement we conclude that the western women liked their men folks a little rough. It may explain the tenacity with which Lydia stuck to Lewis' trail. Probably like the fair Desdemona she "loved him for the dangers he had passed". And like the swarthy Moor he failed to appreciate her.

"Come," continued his mother. "Let your mother fix it up between you two. You surely can't refuse a woman such a trifle. What do you say?"

Dwelling house on the Wetzel Homestead as it appears today. In the foundation of this house are stones taken from the foundation of the Wetzel cabin. This house stands about twenty-five yards from the spot where the cabin stood. It is owned and occupied by E. J. Wilson and family.

"Who is she?" questioned Lewis.

"Why Lydia Boggs, of course," replied the matchmaker.

Wetzel smiled but said nothing as he took his departure. The argument apparently fell on barren soil as far as Lewis was concerned, for he took no steps to carry out his mother's advice. His prison experience in New Orleans seemed to prey on his mind. He felt that he had been wronged, and according to his code a wrong demanded revenge. He told one man that now since he was at home he felt like an arrant coward and longed to return to New Orleans and repay the man and woman who had caused his imprisonment. The more he thought it over the more determined he was to go. Neither the advice of friends nor the "You shan't go" from Lydia could restrain him, so final-

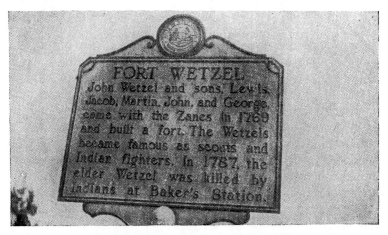

Highway marker of Fort Wetzel as it is today. The dates are both wrong, as the settlement was in 1764 or 1767, and the murder of Captain John was in 1786, as proved by court records.

ly he disappeared to redeem his honor in the only way he knew.

Months passed, but no word from the scout reached Wheeling. Friends feared he had met death in a street brawl, in which his quick temper might easily involve him, while the style of the times would make such an encounter easy to obtain. They had no fear of his ability to take care of himself in the wilderness, but were less sure of his ability in the haunts of men.

Unschooled in books and the ways of towns our hero

was an easy victim of unscrupulous men, but he was highly educated in the ways of the woods and well trained for the occupation of scout.

As recounted in Chapter XII, Lewis Wetzel was easily hoodwinked by scalawags, but he asked no odds of any man when it came to woodcraft. An example of his skill in this art is seen in an event which took place during his stay in Wheeling before his second excursion to the South.

"A man by the name of Mike Forshay turned up at the settlement and entertained the populace by tales of his scouting activities. He admitted that he was good at the business, in fact was rather annoying by his abundant self praise. His favorite topic was how great an Indian hunter he was. One day seeing Lewis Wetzel, whom he did not know, he inquired who that shaggy-looking person was. A by-stander answered that it was some green mountaineer.

Forshay proceeded to develop his favorite topic and offered to bet that no man, red or white, could approach him in the woods without Forshay first seeing him. Lewis Wetzel took him up by saying, "I'll bet the liquor for the crowd that I can come upon you in the woods and touch you on the shoulder without you knowing that I am near until I touch you. Also I will let you name which shoulder I am to touch."

Forshay, being as fond of liquor as he was of boasting, accepted the challenge. A site for the test was selected along the creek some four miles from town. There was a cleared field and a high bank in front, so that Forshay had only three sides to watch. Three judges were chosen and stationed near Forshay.

At a signal Wetzel disappeared in the woods, while Forshay and the judges waited his approach. All was quiet. Not a leaf stirred, not a twig snapped, no trembling bushes pointed to the path of the scout, when suddenly there was Lewis Wetzel with his hand on Forshay's right shoulder.

"You beat me that time, but you can't do it again," exclaimed the Irishman.

"It will be easier next time, and I will show you," replied Lewis, nothing loath to repeat the show.

Again the signal was given, and again his friendly woods swallowed the wraith-like scout. Judges and Forshay kept their eyes peeled in all directions to detect the skulking white man. And once more they neither saw nor heard him until he tapped his victim on the right shoulder. This settled the argument, also Forshay's self-praise. Nothing more was heard about his skill as an Indian hunter. Only

The X in the foreground marks the spot where the original Wetzel cabin stood. It is near Big Wheeling Creek in Marshall County, W. Va.

a Wetzel could negotiate the dry leaves and brush with the stealth necessary to turn this difficult trick.[96]

This exhibition only verified the high opinion everyone who knew him held of Wetzel's woodcraft, so it is no wonder that no fear of his safety was felt when he was in his beloved wilderness. But his reputation for safe conduct among men being quite the opposite it is only natural that folks about gave him up for lost when he did not return

96. From J. H. Newton's "History of the Panhandle."

from New Orleans after several months.   Lydia as usual had faith that she would see him again, and as usual she was right, for with no more warning than he gave Forshay he turned up at Wheeling, his rifle over his shoulder, as though he had only been on one of his hunts.

As to his success on the trip we can only guess, for he told no one about it.   That is no one ever made it public. He may have told Miss Boggs, but if so she showed that at least one woman could keep a secret.   However, since he evinced no irresistible desire to return South, we may deduct that he had settled all scores in that territory.

CHAPTER XIV

Lewis' Second Return from the Southwest and to Lydia at Wheeling

CHANGES occur rapidly in a new country. Already pleasant cottages were replacing stockades and dismantled blockhouses. For the generation of pathfinders the "good old days" were in the rear. The toehold of the struggling Whites along the border had become a firm foothold. Rarely was a redskin seen around the upper Ohio River settlements and the occupation of an Indian hunter was gone in that vicinity.

A change had also taken place in the outlook of Lewis Wetzel. His years in prison had racked his nerves, impaired his health and wreaked even more havoc on his pride. He was still a hunter, as the chase was his only trade. But he renounced the redskin for the more abundant deer, finding a ready demand for the deer hides he brought to town. With the passing years he seemed to regard the taking of life with more thought, and while losing none of his hatred for the red race did not exert himself toward its destruction. Yet the hatchet was not buried.

Returning one day from a hunt in Ohio, tired and suspecting no trouble in the locality where he had spent a week or more, he suddenly glimpsed an Indian raising his gun to fire. Both red and white man dodged behind trees where they remained in suspense for an hour.

To put an end to the deadlock Wetzel hit on a plan he felt pretty sure would work, but which he hesitated to adopt; for perhaps the first time in his life he faltered where an Indian's life was in the balance. But this was a case of self-defense.

"I cannot help myself," said Lewis. Peeping from behind his tree he saw the redman doing the same, but the latter had lodged his gun in a knot of his tree, aimed toward Wetzel's shelter. The scout took off his bearskin cap, stuck it on his hamrod and craftily pushed it in sight of the redman. It brought instant results as the redskin fired

Lewis Wetzel's Cave[97]

97. About 1783 the safety of the white man around Wheeling depended on the keen eyesight, ear alertness and speed afoot. Indians roamed the woods and trails with nothing more to do than to scalp an unsuspecting straggler. It was therefore a common thing for a white man to run and outdistance an Indian, climb a tree and hide in the dense foliage. Wetzel, different from the rest, dug himself a cave, near an Indian trail, on what is known as "tunnel green" east of Wheeling, along Wheeling Creek.

He would hide in this cave which was entirely concealed at that time. When the Indians came along the trail Wetzel could pick them off. He killed eleven braves from the mouth of this cave. He also rushed from his cave and captured several Indian women and children when they would be traveling along the trail nearby. Lewis Wetzel never killed the women and children, but sometimes he would give them to the commander at Fort Henry (which was first known as Fort Fincastle) at Wheeling. In this way they were usually ransomed for captured Whites. Lewis Wetzel would also make a noise like the gobble of a wild turkey to draw the Indians near enough to shoot them.

at what he thought was the paleface's head. The cap sailed through the air, carried by the force of the bullet.

Wetzel leaped in the open and the savage gasped, "White man's ghost!" At this Lewis laughed. The Indian realizing that his opponent was of the flesh and blood variety prepared to hurl his tomahawk, just as the bullet from Wetzel's rifle found its mark. The Indian's weapon fell harmless behind him.

Gazing on the fallen warrior Lewis pondered: "Was my life given me to do such work as this? Are there not nobler ways of dealing with a deadly foe?" The remorseless hunter had become the saddened philosopher; the events of his violent life passed through his puzzled mind. What did his months in prison surrounded by the dregs of society teach him? Had he but his life to live over again! Had he listened to his mother and his sweetheart! If his father had lived, what then? What if his father had been content to dwell in the Lancaster county home, with no future and no fears? What of Lewis' own years of revenge for that father's death? Had his very diligence carried him too far?

While he knew he had meant well, he also felt that this dead Indian before him had possibilities that no man could limit or gauge. It was confusing, and the heart of Wetzel was touched, as it had been by the little Indian girl whose life he tried to save. He trudged on with a new determination in his mind, that of peace if he could obtain it.[98]

That night he called on Lydia and told her of his love.

"Lewis," said she. "Tell me the truth. Were you guilty of the crimes of counterfeiting and intrigue in New Orleans that they imprisoned you for?"

"I have never told any one," said Lewis. "But I will tell you the truth. I am innocent of those crimes, but I killed the Indian they accused me of at Fort Harmar."

---

98.   From Henry C. Watson's *"Six Nights In a Blockhouse,"* and R. C. V. Myer's *"Wetzel the Scout".*

Lewis then spoke of going to the Southwest again.

"Are you going to take me with you?" asked the girl.

"Yes, if you will go with me," he replied.

"But stay here at Wheeling," she urged.

"I'll think about it," said the scout. And thinking about it seemed about the best he could do. He had no trouble in coming to an instant decision in case of emergency on the warpath, but he could not decide when it came to choosing between a home and the open trail.

Wetzel's reputation had long been established. He was proficient in his occupation and was universally regarded as one of the most efficient scouts and practical woodsmen of his day. This was a trade in much demand. Settlers of many nationalities were coming through, anxious to find their claims farther West. The services of the scout were eagerly sought.

Lewis Wetzel was coming down Wheeling Creek one day from one of his Indian hunts and found a large Indian fast in the quicksand in Wheeling Creek opposite the mouth of Wolf Run. The more he struggled the deeper he sank. Wetzel watched him a moment and a bullet from "Old kill nigger" soon put the Indian out of his misery.[99]

Wetzel also had a running fight with a large party of Indians near Kausooth on Fish Creek, in Marshall County, W. Va. He was pursued by six Indians and after Wetzel received a slight wound he succeeded in killing three of them and the other three escaped. Wetzel made a large leap across a stream that astonished the three remaining Indians and caused them to retreat.[100]

Mrs. Scott, a daughter of a Mr. Kelly related this story in the following way to Lewis Bonnett as Lewis Wetzel told her:

"In 1783, Lewis Wetzel and a comrade went over the

---

99. From Mildred Jones' *"History of Viola Community,"* Marshall Co., W. Va.

100. From Guy Mason's *"History of Big Run Community,"* Marshall Co., W. Va.

Ohio river and up Indian Wheeling Creek to what was called the Big Springs. While they were there the Indians fired on them and killed Wetzel's companion. Wetzel fired and killed one Indian, he then took to his heels with five Indians after him. He soon had his gun loaded again, and as one Indian came close upon him waving his tomahawk, Wetzel turned on his heel and shot him dead. He again took to his heels loading his gun as he ran. He was running through a thicket and a bush caught the cock of his gun and tore off the flintlock; which rendered the gun useless to him. He then made with all speed to a branch of the stream with a deep gulley and thick grass. Lewis quickly concealed his gun there to prevent the Indians from getting it. He then headed for the river with all possible speed, and plunged into it above Wheeling island. He swam quarterly down the stream. Three Indians appeared on the bank waving their tomahawks and yelling, as they, too, had left their guns behind in order to overtake Wetzel. They looked very intently at Wetzel in the river, and soon the fourth Indian came to the bank with his gun in his hand. Lewis watched the movements of the last Indian taking aim at him. Wetzel then dived under the water as the Indian pulled the trigger and the bullet harmlessly splashed the water about him. Lewis soon appeared on the upper point of the Island and effected his escape to Fort Henry on the Virginia shore."[101]

"Old Captain Samuel Davis stated that he and Lewis Wetzel went down the Ohio River in March, 1799, with others employed by Jeremiah Kindal to hunt, as Kindal was an Orleans trader from Brownsville, Pa., on the Monongahela River. They went as far as New Madrid on the Mississippi. A great portion of their meat spoiled and some was thrown away. They stayed there all summer, fall and winter. During their hunting excursions at the mouth of the Ohio River the Indians took Lewis Wetzel prisoner.

---

101. Bonnett to Draper, *Draper's Mss.*, 11E83 and 11E84 in the State Historical Society of Wisconsin, Madison, Wisconsin.

They kept him tied two days until Kindal arrived and gave
them some powder for his release. They then proceeded
on until within sixty miles above New Madrid where they
stopped to hunt. Each one took a man with him to carry
in the meat he expected to kill. Davis killed two buffaloes
late one evening, and was forced to stay by them in the
woods all night as they were too far away to get back to
camp that night. Lewis Wetzel who had been hunting in
another direction returned and told Kindal that 300 Indians
were approaching the camp. Kindal ordered all to follow
him and getting all the boats they moved down the river
about six miles, leaving Davis and his man behind.

"When Davis returned the next day and found them
gone he and his man proceeded at once to build a raft and
follow them down the river. In turning around a bluff the
raft struck some driftwood. The man got excited, jumped
off the raft onto a log and got to shore safely but was never
heard of afterwards. Davis by much difficulty got his raft
out in the current, and was driven by its force on a cotton-
wood island. He was confined there three days and two
nights without one mouthful of food. He had taken some
meat on the raft with him but the waves in a gale of wind
washed it away. At last Davis luckily found a canoe on
the lower end of the island sticking in a driftwood pile.
After much hard work and with a great hazard of life from
the waves and storm he finally reached Kindal and his
party.

"There was considerable altercation between Davis and
Kindal about his leaving Davis behind, but when Kindal
told him it was Wetzel's fault that they left him behind,
because of the approaching Indians, that settled it. The
party then moved on to New Madrid. When they got to
New Madrid they missed Wetzel and sent a file of men
after him.

"On the way down Wetzel disappeared from the party,
slipped into the woods and waited for a boat going down

the river. He boarded the first one that came along and went to New Orleans."[102]

"It was in the month of February that Captain Samuel Davis and one named Campbell went up the Big Sandusky river to trap beaver. They both were made prisoners by the Indians and Davis was doomed to be burned at the stake.

"They both effected their escape one night and took with them all the horses that the Indians had stolen in Kentucky, a few weeks before. The horses had been turned out the evening before on the opposite side of the stream from the camp. Davis and his companion crossed the stream, secured the horses and escaped to Kentucky and returned the horses to their owners who rewarded them well."[103]

---

102. Bonnett to Draper, *Draper's Mss.*, 11E85 and 11E86 in the State Historical Society of Wisconsin, Madison, Wisconsin.
103. Bonnett to Draper, *Draper's Mss.*, 11E86 in the State Historical Society of Wisconsin, Madison, Wisconsin.

CHAPTER XV

THE land south of the Ohio River had been granted to the Whites by a treaty with the Indians, but all the Indians did not sign the treaty. Those who did not sign did not honor the agreement, on the grounds that those who signed had no authority over them. It is also possible that some of the signers regretted their bargain and chose to look on the agreement as a "scrap of paper".

The settlers naturally felt that they were in the right when taking up this land and making homes there. The Indians, on the other hand, had formed a confederation of tribes in Ohio headed by Joseph Brant for the purpose of stopping the encroachments of Whites. The situation was full of dynamite, and it exploded at slight provocation.

In the spring of 1790 six voyagers, four men and two women, [104] set out down the Ohio to Limestone, now Maysville, Ky. Near the mouth of the Scioto two white men ran down the bank in great excitement and begged the travelers to take them on board, as they had escaped Indians who were hot after them. The voyagers, however, were suspicious of a trap and continued to drift with the current, meanwhile arguing whether to take a chance on rescuing the supposed escaped Whites.

Eventually one man named Flinn could not bear the idea of abandoning two of his race to the savages and insisted that he be put ashore and that the boat then push off

---

104. How things often worked out when settlers went to occupy this promised land is illustrated by the account of "May's Disastrous Trip Down the Ohio," as told by H. A. Bruce in *Daniel Boone and the Wilderness Road*.

and continue until he determined whether the two on shore were escaping from Indians or trying to lure the others to their fate.

The minute he leaped on the bank a half dozen redskins seized him and then commenced firing on the boat, which could not get away very fast. They killed two on the boat and then boarded the craft, shaking hands all around as they did so. Having shaken hands cordially with the live whites they proceeded coolly to scalp the dead ones. Then they found a barrel of rum, and the party was complete so far as they were concerned.

Next morning three boat-loads of Virginia gentlemen came down the river. Here was another prize, which the Indians made for with all the speed they could get out of their white captives, whom they drafted into rowing. The Virginians escaped only by abandoning two of their boats and all their goods and horses to the enemy.

Flinn, the man whose kindness of heart gave the redskins the chance they were waiting for, was finally burned at the stake. Stiles, another of those captured, ran the gauntlet and was condemned to death, but made his escape and reached the settlements. Miss Fleming, one of the women, was rescued by a chief when she was bound to a stake for the final ceremony, and conducted to Pittsburgh. The other woman was killed when the redmen first fired on the boat. At that time May, the leader, while in the act of waving his nightcap as a token of surrender was shot in the forehead. The remaining man, Johnson, was captured, later ransomed by the French and returned to his family.

Thus we see that a trip down the Ohio was not a pleasure excursion those days. The settlers had to fight to get to their lands, fight to hold them, then work themselves half to death to keep from starving entirely. The help of a Wetzel was right welcome in this active occupation, and he turned his energies toward helping these home-hungry folks get located.

Lewis Wetzel's presence with a group was a protection against hostile redmen, for his fame had permeated the Indian stamping grounds. The redskins feared him and seemed to give those in his care a wide berth. It is even likely that they feared he was on their trail when he was not, and that this wholesome respect tempered their activities.

Presley Martin related the following story to Sylvester Myers:

"My grandfather, John Martin, came to Wheeling from New Jersey, in the early days. When John was a young lad he once took a scout with Lewis Wetzel down the Ohio River. When they arrived at a point a short distance below where Proctor, W. Va., now stands, it was getting late in the evening, and they began to look about for a favorable spot to spend the night. Wetzel, as was his custom before settling down for the night took a circle around to see that everything was safe, for the Indians occasionally crossed over from Ohio into West Virginia. About the time Wetzel rounded into the center a big raccoon jumped up against the side of a tree and young Martin shot it. While they were feeling it and remarking how fat it was and what a fine mess it would make, Wetzel suddenly sprang up, with his gun in his hand, as though he had been told, and said, 'Indians, Martin'. He took another circuit and found fresh signs of Indians. The two held a hurried consultation, as to fight or try to escape. It was decided to start for the Wheeling fort, as Wetzel did not want to expose young Martin to the Indians. On their return, Wetzel took a run and leaped the mouth of Proctor creek at one bound, a distance of 21 feet. Martin was compelled to swim across as the water was too deep to wade. John Martin related that this was the liveliest night's travel that he ever had in his life."[105]

---

105. From Sylvester Myer's *"History of West Virginia."*

CHAPTER XVI

Last Days Along the Frontier for Lewis Wetzel

AMONG those interested in western lands was John Madison, brother of James, who later became President of the United States. Madison hired Lewis Wetzel to go with him through the Kanawha region, now in West Virginia. On this trip they ran across a deserted hunter's camp where they found some goods concealed. "I think I'll help myself to a blanket," said Madison, and he did so.

In crossing the Little Kanawha that day they were fired on and Madison killed.[106] The change in Wetzel's mind is seen here in that he did not pursue the redman who fired the fatal shot, but took Madison's body to friends in Wheeling.

From then on he spent most of his time in the woods, not as a relentless hunter of Indians or even wild animals, but in communion with the birds and the beasts which seemed to know him as a friend. It is said that a delicate, lame doe used to come and rest its face beside that of the one-time fierce destroyer, unafraid. But we are afraid that here again the zeal of the historian has carried him beyond established facts. Let us put it down beside other accounts to help balance the score.

When in 1804 Lewis and Clark started on their historic

---

106. Bonnett told Draper that Lewis Wetzel was employed as a chain carrier to survey land with Madison. Also that another man was killed the same time that Madison was killed. An Indian pursued Lewis and he had to kill him in order to save his own scalp. Wetzel whirled and shot him as the Indian was chasing him. Bonnett related that Lewis Wetzel told him this with his own mouth. Bonnett to Draper, *Draper's Mss.*, 11E93 and 24S63 in the State Historical Society of Wisconsin, Madison, Wisconsin.

trip across the Rockies the fame of Lewis Wetzel in Kentucky marked him as a man useful in their enterprise. They sent a messenger to him and he finally consented to join them. He spent four months with the party, then came back home, because the trip was too slow and not exciting enough for him.

Apparently this excursion renewed his old restlessness, and he decided to see strange lands for himself again. He bade his mother and sisters good-bye. When he came to Lydia she asked, "When shall you return?"

"We need you here," said Lydia. "And besides you promised to take me with you."

"If I find a place that suits me to settle I will send for you or come for you—if you will marry me then."

This was Lydia's turn to hang back, and we can hardly blame her. Moses Shepherd had become a candidate for her affections. So she countered with Lewis' former words: "I will think about it."

Lewis defended his decision to go South by saying: "I do not think I am needed here at Wheeling any longer, since the new civilization has come about. The Indians are so peaceful and quiet that killing them would be nothing short of murder. They may be fiercer and wilder farther West, but I shall not go there. I am getting too old."

"Old! You old at forty years of age?" cried the girl.

"I have lived more than my age in many things," said the sober and truthful scout. Stubborn as usual he took passage on a flat-boat down the river. His friends gathered to see him off. Among them were Bertha Madison and her husband and Simon Bonnett's wife, whom he had helped rescue from the redmen. His mother was there and said, "The world is wide, but it always sends us back to where we started. Good-bye, my son. And come again in the spring."

"Let's give three cheers!" said Moses Shepherd, rival for Lydia's hand and at least one of the crowd who could endure Wetzel's absence very well.

"Don't you dare!" spoke Lydia. "He is not going out in happiness. Can't you see his face, and the sorrow there?"

"I am glad to see him going, but I wish him well," said the honest Moses.

The boat cast off, was pushed into the stream, caught by the current and drifted down the river, the ripples from its passage patting softly on the shore.

Down past heavy shadows a ray of sunlight turned the tireless river into limpid gold. Into this strip of molten beauty sailed the flat-boat, and a shaft of sunlight found a figure standing at the prow. It lit the dark face until it

Lydia Boggs, (Courtesy, The Wheeling News-Register)

glowed with a strange expression, while the gun-barrel threw flashes of reflected sunlight as the gently rocking boat diverted the angle of incidence. With hat held aloft as a parting signal the figure stood on the boat and like another Hiawatha sailed away in a blaze of sunlight until the boat rounded a curve and hid him from view. The ripples from the boat lapping the shore at their feet told his friends that he was gone, but they failed to whisper that he would not return.

Lewis Wetzel never came back. For a while he was heard

from by Lydia and his mother, for whom he now seemed to have more consideration than he showed earlier in life. Then no word came.

Moses Shepherd pressed his suit, but the faithful Lydia awaited the coming of Lewis to take her to a new home in the South. She waited in vain.

At Natchez, Mississippi, Lewis visited his cousin Philip Sikes, (or Sycks). Here he contracted a fever and in the summer of 1808[107] died, aged 44 years. He was buried in a small cemetery about 20 miles from Natchez.[108-109-110]

Lewis Wetzel's grave about twenty miles from Natchez and verified by George Wetzel, son of Martin Wetzel, Lewis' oldest brother.

107.   Bonnett to Draper, *Draper's Mss.*, 24S62 in the State Historical Society of Wisconsin, Madison, Wisconsin.
108.   David McIntire of Belmont County, Ohio, was the last man from the vicinity of Wheeling to have seen Lewis Wetzel. He saw him at Natchez, where he was on a visit in 1808. This is verified by George Wetzel, son of Martin Wetzel, Lewis' brother.
109.   Some narratives say that Lewis Wetzel married a French lady, settled some distance up the Arkansas river, and died there in 1829. Lyman C. Draper does not have any faith in this story.
110.   The Texas Historical Association says that Lewis Wetzel died at Texas-on-the-Brazos in 1830 at the age of 67 years while visiting his cousin David Sikes (or Sycks). Bonnett and Draper do not have faith in this account.

Lydia Boggs eventually married Moses Shepherd [111] it is said, and lived at Wheeling until her death, which occurred in 1872. [112]

Wetzel was a product of his times, and like many another pathfinder achieved honor or renown by skill in

---

111. Moses Shepherd was the youngest son of Colonel David Shepherd and Rachel Teague. He was born in Shepherdstown, Va., November 11, 1763. His only brother was killed at the siege of Fort Henry, September 1, 1777. He had three sisters. Elizabeth married Major William McIntire, the paymaster of Forts Henry and Shepherd; Sarah married Francis Duke; and Ruth, the youngest sister, married Captain John Mills, who was given a land grant where they lived and were buried, which is now known as Chantal Court. Moses Shepherd was the great-great-grandson of John Van Meter, the "Indian trader", the first White man to cross the Blue Ridge; great-grandson of John Van Meter, called "John the First of Berkeley", who, with his brother Isaac, received the grant of 40,000 acres of land from Governor Gooch in 1730; the grandson of Captain Thomas Shepherd, founder of Shepherdstown, Va. Moses Shepherd proved himself a worthy descendant of these pioneers.

Moses was seven or eight years old when his father moved his large family to the plantation lying between Big Wheeling and Little Wheeling and lying beyond Middle Wheeling Creek. On a beautiful site near the bank of Big Wheeling Creek, Fort Shepherd was built by Colonel David Shepherd. This fort became the refuge of the neighborhood. After seven years Fort Shepherd was destroyed by the Indians, and Colonel Shepherd was ordered by General Hand to take command of Fort Henry. He moved his family there, including the husbands of his daughters and their children. In the siege of Fort Henry the women and girls shared the work of defending the fort, loaded the guns, made the ammunition and burned their hands with hot bullets. After the siege Moses went with his father to Catfish Camp, Pa., where he remained five years. During these years he made frequent visits to the plantation and helped restore the buildings, including Fort Shepherd.

In 1798 he built upon the site of Fort Shepherd the handsome stone mansion now called the "Shepherd Mansion," "The Stone House," and now, "Monument Place".

The last and perhaps the most important work of Moses Shepherd's life was his connection in the building of the Cumberland road, now called the National road or U. S. 40, by constructing several miles of this road and building several bridges.

This National road is the only highway of its kind ever constructed by the United States government. Henry Clay was the chief advocate in Congress for funds to build this road which was the bond of sympathy that united Henry Clay and Moses Shepherd into a firm friendship. Moses Shepherd and Lydia Boggs Shepherd his wife, had a fine monument erected to Henry Clay near the "Monument Place" to commemorate his distinguished public services on behalf of the National road. *History of the Panhandle*, by J. H. Newton, 1879.

(Continued on page 200)

woodcraft and courage in warfare. He was a decided force in helping to settle this territory and while he had no plans or schemes of conquest or expansion, by doing diligently the tasks before him he aided in keeping the natives at a distance until the Whites could establish themselves, while his example of reckless daring and uncanny success was inspiring at a time when the harassed settlers needed all the encouragement they could get.

DeHass, the historian, describes Wetzel as true as the needle to the pole when he professed friendship. "He loved his friends and hated his enemies. He was a rude, blunt man, with few words before company, but with his friends not only sociable but an agreeable companion.

"His name and fame will long survive, when the achievements of men vastly superior in rank and intellect will slumber with the forgotten past. To us he was a desperado. In that day he was considered a great hero."

(Continued from page 199)

112. Lydia Boggs was born in Berkeley County, Virginia, Feb. 26, 1766, and died in 1872 at the age of 106 years. She was the daughter of Captain John Boggs, who moved from Virginia to Chartiers Creek, Pa., and came to Wheeling in 1777. He was also stationed at Catfish Camp, now Washington, Pa., with forty men on Sept. 1, 1777. He was brought to Wheeling after this siege to strengthen the fort. Captain Boggs was sheriff of Ohio County, Va., in 1785. He lived on Buffalo Creek in 1781 and moved back to Wheeling the next year. Lydia accompanied him on all the movements. She remembered well of seeing Lord Dunmore when her father was in charge of Catfish Camp. Moses Shepherd was there at the same time and their acquaintance began young. After her marriage to Colonel Moses Shepherd she accompanied him on various expeditions until his death in 1832. During her frequent visits to Washington, D. C., she met General Cruger, a member of Congress from New York state. They were married in 1833. Lydia was at the second siege of Fort Henry and although but 16 years of age she melted bullets until her arms and hands were blistered. Lewis Wetzel, Betty Zane and Moses Shepherd were in that siege also. Lydia said that Betty Zane did not deserve the credit for saving Fort Henry as Molly Scott really carried the powder that saved the fort.

In 1781 Captain John Boggs and his son William and his daughter Lydia were captured by the Indians on Buffalo Creek. The father and daughter soon escaped but William was a prisoner 18 months before he escaped.

STOUT HEARTED LEWIS WETZEL

Stout hearted Lewis Wetzel
Rides down the river shore,
The wilderness behind him,
The wilderness before.

He rides in the cool of morning,
Humming the dear old tune,
"Into the heart of the greenwood,
Into the heart of June."

He needs no guide in the forest
More than the honey bees;
His guides are the cool green mosses
To the northward of the trees.

Nor fears him the foe whose footstep
Is light as the summer air;
His tomahawk hangs in his shirt belt,
The scalp knife glitters there.

The stealthy Wyandottes tremble
And speak his name with fear,
For his aim is sharp and deadly,
And his rifle's ring is clear.

So pleasantly rides he onward,
Pausing to hear the stroke
Of the settler's axe in the forest,
Or the crack of a falling oak.

The partridge drums on the dry oak,
The croaking croby crows,
The blackbird sings in the spice bush,
The robin in the haws.

And as they chatter and twitter,
    The wild bird seems to say:
"Do not harm us, good Lewis,
    And you shall have luck to-day."

A sharp clear ring through the greenwood,
    And with mightier leap and bound,
The pride of the western forest
    Lies bleeding on the ground.

Then out from the leafy shadows
    A stalwart hunter springs,
And his unsheathed scalp knife glittering,
    Against his rifle rings.

"And who art thou," quoth Lewis,
    "That comest twixt me and mine?"
And his cheek is flushed with anger,
    As a bacchant's flushed with wine.

"What boots that to thy purpose?"
    The stranger hot replies;
"My rifle marked it living,
    And mine, when dead, the prize."

Then with sinewy arms they grapple,
    Like giants fierce in brawls,
Till stretched along greensward
    The humble hunter falls.

"Now take this rod of alder,
    Set it by yonder tree
A hundred yards beyond me
    And wait you there and see."

"For he who dares such peril
    But lightly hold his breath,

May his unshrieved soul be ready
To welcome sudden death."

So the stranger takes the alder,
And wandering stands in view,
While Wetzel's aim grows steady
And he cuts the rod in two.

"By heavens," exclaims the stranger,
"One only, far and nigh,
Hath arms like the lithe young ash tree
Or half so keen an eye."

"And that is Lewis Wetzel."
Quoth Lewis. "Here he stands."
So they speak in gentle manner
And clasp their friendly hands.

Ride out of the leafy greenwood,
As rises the yellow moon,
And the purple hills lie pleasantly
In the softened air of June. [113]

FLOHUS B. PIMPTON.

Used by permission.

113.   Wetzel County, West Virginia, is named for Lewis Wetzel. State route 7 through Wetzel County, W. Va., was named the "Lewis Wetzel Trail", by the West Virginia legislature in the 1937 session.

THE BALLAD OF LEWIS WETZEL

By Glen Baker

My parents came from sturdy stock,
  They were tall brown people and merry,
With the keen eyesight of the soaring hawk
  And lips like the redhaw berry.

Horny-handed folk inured to toil,
  They marched in the pioneer legion
To carve a home from the virgin soil
  Of Virginia's farthermost region.

And I was born on the Wilderness Road
  In a tawny sunlit clearing,
I cut my teeth on an oxen goad
  And had a backwoods rearing.

And I remember the cabin there
  In the clearing on the Big Wheeling,
The coarse but wholesome pioneer fare
  And the herbs that hung from the ceiling.

And childhood years when days were long
  And the first spring winds were blowing,
My mother humming an old Welsh song
  As my father bent to his hoeing.

And then one day the Indians came
  With their inhuman yells and laughter,
And our cabin blazed with rifle flame
  And smoke went up to the rafters.

But the walls were staunch and the red men fled
  And the days flowed on as before,

Till I grew too tall for a trundle bed
And I slept on the puncheon floor.

And so I came to my tall manhood
With a woodman's knowledge and daring,
And so with a rifle for livelihood
I started my forest faring.

And once as I turned the homeward way
I crossed the trail of some savages,
And hurried on through the dying day
Sensing a scene of red ravages.

And when I came to the clearing there
Where the path of maize was greening,
I saw my mother tearing her hair
And waking the woods with her keening.

And my father's form so still and cold
With the riven skull that was hairless,
All that remained of a loved household
Shattered by red hands and careless.

And over the grave we dug that night
In the raw rich frontier clay,
I swore an oath to harry and blight
The red race by night and day.

I swore it there as the forest gloomed
Forbidding and dark in its silence,
A savage oath that forever doomed
Us all to a life of violence.

And many a red brave homeward bound
From the latest scene of his pillage,
Heard in the forest a moaning sound
And died within sight of his village.

For thus I played on the red man's fear
  As I blew through my rifle bore,
Warning him when his end was near
  With the "Deathwind" of border lore.

And down the years I kept my vow
  Till the red tribes, westward turning,
Left this valley to settler and plow
  And freedom from pillage and burning.

And time rolled on and my breath was stilled
  And they laid me away to the long rest,
But even in death my spirit willed
  To continue on with the long quest.

So still I follow the trail of the braves
  And wraithlike still I go stealing
Over the lands the Ohio laves
  From Cincinnati to the Big Wheeling.

And on autumn nights when dark winds carol
  And thunderstorms roll and rally,
You can hear me blow through my rifle barrel
  The length of the Ohio Valley.[114]

---

114. From the March, 1939, issue of the *National Historical Magagzine,* published by the National Society of the Daughters of the American Revolution.

BIBLIOGRAPHY

Primary Sources of Information

Bonnett's, Lewis, Letters to Lyman C. Draper, 1845 to 1850, of the State Historical Society of Wisconsin, Madison, Wisconsin.

Draper's, Lyman C., Letters to Lewis Bonnett, 1845 to 1850, of the State Historical Society of Wisconsin, Madison, Wisconsin.

Draper's, Lyman C., Manuscripts in the State Historical Society of Wisconsin, Madison, Wisconsin.

Bowers, George W., *Original and Photostatic Papers and Documents*, Mannington, West Virginia.

Caldwell, Harry, *Original Papers and Documents*, Pine Hill, West Virginia.

Dague, Carrie M., *Original Papers and Documents*, Elm Grove, West Virginia.

Manuscripts in the Library of the Virginia Historical Society, Richmond, Virginia.

Manuscripts in the Land Office of Virginia, Richmond, Va.

Manuscripts in the Berks County Historical Society of Pennsylvania, Reading, Pennsylvania.

Records in the Clerk of the County Court's Office in the Courthouse at Wheeling, Ohio County, West Virginia.

Records in the Clerk of the County Court's Office in the Courthouse at Moundsville, Marshall County, W. Va.

Allman, Clarence B., *The Life and Times of Lewis Wetzel*, Mennonite Publishing House of Scottdale, Pa. 1932.

Hartley, Cecil B., *The Life of Lewis Wetzel*, G. G. Evans, Philadelphia, Pennsylvania, 1860.

Myers, R. C. V., *Wetzel the Scout*. Hurst and Company, New York City, N. Y., 1883.

208   THE LIFE AND TIMES OF LEWIS WETZEL

Secondary Sources of Information

Bruce, H. A., *Daniel Boone and The Wilderness Road.*

Frost, John, *Thrilling Adventures Among the Indians.* Published by J. W. Bradley, Philadelphia, Pa., 1851.

Pritt, J., *Mirrors of Oldentime Border Life,* Abingdon, Virginia, 1849.

Howe, Henry *Historical Collections of Ohio,* Vols. I and II, Cincinnati, Ohio, 1888.

Watson, Henry C., *Six Nights in a Blockhouse.* Hurst and Company, New York City, N. Y., 1880.

Withers, Alexander Scott, *Chronicles of Border Warfare,* Joseph Israel, Clarksburg, Virginia, 1831. Reprint by Stewart and Kidd, Cincinnati, Ohio, and edited by Reuben Gold Thwaites, 1895.

Hildreth, Samuel B., *Pioneer History of America,* Vol. I, Cincinnati, Ohio, 1842.

Newton, James H., *History of The Panhandle,* Wheeling, West Virginia, 1879.

Powell, W. Scott, *History of Marshall County,* Cincinnati, Ohio, 1925.

Powell, W. Scott, *"Footsteps of Civilization,"* Vols. I and II. Bound but not Printed. In the Moundsville Public Library at Moundsville, West Virginia.

Myers, Sylvester R., *History of West Virginia,* Vols. I and II. News Publishing Company, Wheeling, W. Va., 1915.

Bennett, Emerson, *Forrest Rose.* Outcalt and Company, Lancaster, Ohio, 1861.

DeHass, Wills, *History of the Early Settlements and Indian Wars of Western Virginia, Previous to 1795.* Wheeling, Virginia, 1851.

Jacob, John G., *Life and Times of Patrick Gass.* Wellsburg, Virginia, 1859.

Wiley, Samuel T., *History of Preston County, West Virginia.* Kingwood, West Virginia, 1883.

Brant and Fuller, *History of the Upper Ohio Valley,* Vols. I and II. Madison, Wisconsin, 1891.

Nowland, John H. B., *Prominent Citizens of Indianapolis*, Vol. I. Indianapolis, Ind., 1877.

Nowland, John H. B., *Early Reminiscences of Indianapolis, 1820 to 1876*. Indianapolis, Ind., 1877.

Blanchard, ————, *History of Morgan County, Indiana*. Indianapolis, Indiana, 1880.

Bates, Samuel P., *History of Greene County, Pennsylvania*. Nelson, Rishforth and Company, Chicago, Ill., 1888.

Thwaites, Reuben G., and Kellogg, L. P., *Dunmore's War*. Democrat Publishing Company. The State Historical Society of Wisconsin, Madison, Wisconsin, 1905.

Thwaites, Reuben G., and Kellogg, L. P., *Frontier Defense of the Upper Ohio*. Castle-Pierce Printing Company. The State Historical Society of Wisconsin, Madison, Wisconsin, 1912.

McKnight, Charles, *Our Western Border One Hundred Years Ago*, Philadelphia, Pennsylvania, 1876.

Doddridge, Joseph, *Notes on the Settlement and Indian Wars in Western Parts of Virginia and Pennsylvania, 1763-1783*. Wellsburg, Virginia, 1824; Albany, New York, 1876; Pittsburgh, Pennsylvania, 1912; Strasburg, Virginia, 1925.

————, *Pioneer Life in the West*. Philadelphia, Pennsylvania, 1861.

McEldowney, John C., Jr. *History of Wetzel County*. New Martinsville, West Virginia, 1901.

Pennsylvania Archives, Third Series, Vols. I, II, III, and XVIII. Philadelphia, Pennsylvania.

Hardesty, ————, *History of Marshall, Ohio, Wirt and Calhoun Counties*. 1883-1884.

John Wetzel's Muster Roll

Pay Abstract of Captain John Whitsell's (now Wetzel's), company of Rangers, Monongahela and Ohio Counties under command of Colonel Daniel McFarland. Ranging in Monongahela and Ohio Counties from the 22nd day of

April to the 25th day of July, 1778, both days included:

John Whitsell, Captain
William Crawford, Lieutenant
John Madison, Ensign
Peter Miller, Sergeant
Christian Copley, Sergeant
John Province, Jr., Quartermaster

Privates were:

John Six	Samuel Brown
Lewis Bonnett	Jacob Towesbaugh
Joseph Morris	Benjamin Wright
William Hall	Philip Nicholas
John Nicholas	Henry Yoho
John Duncan	Thomas Hargis
Nicholas Crousber	Henry Franks
Jacob Teusbaugh	John Six, Jr.
Abram Eastwood	Conrad Hur
Martin Whitsell (Wetzel)	Enoch Enochs
Jacob Riffle	Mark Hare
Valentine Lawrence	John Andrews
John Smith	William Gardner
David Casto	Joseph Yeager
Philip Catt	George Catt
Joseph Coone	Matthias Riffle
Jacob Spangler	Peter Goosey
Philip Baker	Jacob Liton

The roll is signed by David Brodhead as commander.

The privates received six and two-thirds dollars each for the three months' and five days' service. Stated in continental currency as "7-18-4". The captain received $40 for his three months' and five days' service. His pay was in continental currency "47-10-10." [115]

115. From Samuel Wiley's *History of Monongalia County*, *W. Va.* Kingwood, W. Va. 1883. Page 70.

Reprinted in Thwaites and Kellogg's *Frontier Defense on the Upper Ohio.* Madison, Wisconsin. 1912. Page 305.

From a photostatic copy of the original owned by George W. Bowers, Mannington, W. Va.

APPENDICES

Copy of the first Whitsell (or Wetzel) deed taken from the original owned by Harry Caldwell of Pine Hill, West Virginia:

"Edmund Randolph, Esquire, Governor of the Commonwealth of Virginia. To all to whom these presents shall come, GREETING: Knoe ye that by consideration of a treasurery warrant number Two Thousand Four Hundred and Seventy-Four, issued the Twenty-third of June, 1783. There is granted by the said Commonwealth unto John Whetsel of Richmond a certain tract or parcel of land containing 1,000 acres by survey bearing date the Fifteenth day of July, 1784, and being in the County of Ohio on the waters of Big Wheeling Creek and bounded as follows, to-wit: Beginning at a hickory and sugar tree on the banks of a run and running thence South Four Hundred and Seventy Poles to a white oak; thence East Three Hundred and Forty Poles to a black oak and chestnut; thence North Four Hundred and Seventy Poles to the beginning; with its appurtenances: To have and to hold the said Tract or Parcel of land with its appurtenances to the said John Whetsel and his heirs forever.

In Witness Whereof the said Edmund Randolph, Esquire, Governor of the Commonwealth of Virginia, hath herewith set his hand and caused the lesser seal of the said Commonwealth to be affixed at Richmond, on the Sixteenth day of April in the year of our Lord One Thousand Seven

Hundred and Eighty-Seven and of the Commonwealth the
Eleventh.

Signed, Edmund Randolph.[116-117-118]

Copy of the second grant of land taken from the original in the possession of Carrie M. Dague, of Elm Grove,
West Virginia.

Edmund Randolph, Esquire, Governor of the Commonwealth of Virginia, To all to whom these presents shall
come, GREETING: Knoe Ye, that by virtue and in consideration of a presumption, Treasurery Warrant Number
Two Thousand Four Hundred and Ninety-Eight, issued the
Twenty-third of June, One Thousand Seven Hundred and
Eighty-three.

There is granted by the said Commonwealth unto John
Whetsel a certain Tract of land, containing Five Hundred
Acres, by survey bearing date the Twelfth day of February,
One Thousand Seven Hundred and Eighty-Seven, lying and
being in the County of Ohio, on Big Wheeling Creek and
bounded as follows:

To-wit: Beginning at a Sugar tree standing on the Bank
of Big Wheeling by the mouth of a drain, thence South One
Hundred and Forty Poles to two White Oaks, thence South
Twenty Degrees, East One Hundred and Eighty Poles to a

---

116. On the back of this grant is the following: John Whetsel
is entitled to the Within mentioned tract of land.

John F. Adams, R. S. Off.

117. Survey Book 2, page 9, in the Clerk of the County Court's
Office in the Courthouse at Wheeling, Ohio County, West Virginia,
shows that William Shepherd as assistant to Robert Woods surveyed
500 acres of this tract on February 12, 1787. This land was granted
to John Wetzel as an assignee of Thomas McGuire. It is not known
why the other 500 acres was not surveyed at that time.

118. Survey Book 2, page 260, in the Clerk of the County Court's
Office in the Courthouse at Wheeling, Ohio County, West Virginia,
shows John Williamson as assistant to Robert Woods surveyed 250
acres of land, that was granted to John Wetzel as an assignee of
William English. The land was surveyed on February 1, 1792, and
was granted to John Wetzel June 23, 1783. This tract was on Big
Wheeling Creek in Ohio County, West Virginia.

White Oak, thence South Seventy-One Degrees, thence East One Hundred and Eighteen Poles to a Black Oak, thence North Seventy-two Degrees, East Eighty Poles to a Spanish Oak, N. 15, E. 70 Poles, crossing Wheeling Creek to a Sugar tree, N. 75, W. 80 Poles to a Sycamore on the Bank of the Creek, then down the several Courses and meanders 132 Poles to a Sugar tree, thence leaving said Creek N. 100 Poles crossing Turkey Run to a Sugar and White Oak S. 100 Poles to a White Walnut standing on the Bank of the Creek at the Mouth of Turkey Run, corner to Lawrence Stricker and with his line-up the several Courses and meanders of said Creek crossing the same 88 Poles to the Beginning, with its Appurtenances to the said John Whetsell and his heirs forever.

IN WITNESS whereof the said Edmund Randolph, Governor of the Commonwealth of Virginia, hath hereunto set His Hand, and caused the Lesser Seal of the said Commonwealth to be affixed at Richmond, on the Thirteenth of June in the year of Our Lord, One Thousand Seven Hundred and Eighty-Eight, and of the Commonwealth the Twelfth.

[SEAL]   Edmund Randolph.[119-120-121]

---

119. On the outside of this warrant are these words, "John Whetsell is entitled to the within mentioned tract of land.
                                        John Harris, Rec. Sec."
120. Frederick Dague, great-great-grandfather of Carrie M. Dague, bought 400 acres of the 500 acre Whetsel tract in 1795, 200 of which he willed his son, Frederick H. Dague, who had rented this piece of land from the Whetsells earlier than 1796. Eventually Frederick H. Dague bought the other 200 acres. Until quite recently this 400 acre tract has been in the possession of the Dague family. A portion of it was sold to the Baltimore and Ohio Railroad.
121. Survey Book 2, page 8, in the Clerk of the County Court's Office in the Courthouse at Wheeling, Ohio County, West Virginia, shows that William Shepherd as assistant to Robert Woods, surveyed 400 acres of this tract of land at the mouth of Stulls Run, February 13, 1787. This land was granted to John Wetzel, who was an assignee of Thomas McGuire, by warrant No. 2498. It is not known why the other 100 acres was not included in the survey.

Appraisement of John Wetzel's Personal Property

Inventory of the goods and Chattels of John Wetzel, deceased. Appraised by us the undersigned this 19th day of August, 1786.

	Pounds	Shillings	Pence
One pied cow	3	10	0
One ball cow	3	10	0
One young cow	2	10	0
One white and red cow	3	10	0
One cow and calf	3	10	0
One bull	1	8	0
Two bull calves	1	10	0
Two bull calves	1	10	0
One heifer	1	10	0
One ditto	0	15	0
One calf	0	15	0
One ditto	0	6	0
One ditto	0	6	0
One chestnut mare	10	0	0
One black mare	2	10	0
One sorrel mare	10	0	0
One sorrel colt	3	10	0
One gray colt	3	0	0
One bay mare	10	0	0
One gray horse	7	0	0
One boar	0	6	0
Two sheep	0	16	0
15 hogs	3	2	6
A small cornfield	2	0	0
One small stack of wheat	1	10	0
One iron pot and rack	0	18	0
One ditto	0	14	0
One small pot	0	10	0
One ditto	0	2	0
One skillet	0	4	0
One ditto	0	2	6
One frying pan	0	2	0

	Pounds	Shillings	Pence
One brass kettle	0	10	0
One steel trap	0	4	0
Two small steel traps	0	12	0
One broken ditto	0	3	0
One whip saw	2	0	0
Two coopers' tools	0	10	0
To old iron	0	3	0
To old iron pile, and edge adze	1	4	0
To pickling tub	0	0	30
To one hatchet	0	8	0
Two mattocks, and axes	0	18	0
One pair steelyards	0	8	0
One washing tub	0	4	0
Two axes, wedges, and log chain	1	6	0
Three weeding hoes	0	12	0
Three old iron kettles	0	5	0
One fro; one hoe, and maul ring	0	0	0
One ploy, and clevis	0	0	5
One iron harrow	0	12	0
Two bells	0	4	0
Two grindstones	0	4	0
One loom, and jagger	0	8	0
Two brass kettles	0	8	0
To pewter	2	0	0
Knives and forks	0	3	0
One iron square	0	2	6
One box iron	0	2	6
One old gun	0	10	0
One old gun	0	10	0
One iron swivel	0	2	0
One pair wool combs	0	2	0
One pair saddle bags	0	18	0
One sugar tub	0	2	6
One silver watch	3	0	0
One pair market baskets	1	10	0
Four pair oak baskets	0	3	0

	Pounds	Shillings	Pence
Two books	0	3	0
To his clothes	3	0	0
Three shirts	1	16	0
Three blankets	1	4	0
One half bushel	0	1	0
One feather bed and furniture	1	0	0
To wool	0	4	0
One spinning wheel	0	7	0
To one feather bed	1	4	0
To a box	0	3	0
One leather collar	0	5	0
One old ladder	0	6	0
A quantity of salt	2	14	0
To flax	0	4	0
To leather	0	13	0
To brand iron, tomahawk, and long hoe	0	2	0
One foot adze, and broken clevis	3	3	0
One cow	3	5	0
One calf	0	18	0
One mare	5	10	0
A quantity of fur	11	0	0
A hand mill	0	15	0
To wooden bushels	0	12	0
To one iron kettle	1	10	0
One bake oven	0	12	0
One plow iron	1	0	0
One old axe	0	2	0
One brass kettle	0	10	0
Every excepted			
	140	14	6

Signed,
James McConnell,
Lewis Bonnett,

Lewis Lindhoff,
Martin Collons,
Appraisers.[122]

122. Recorded in Settlement Book No. 1, p. 35 in the Clerk of the County Court's Office in the Courthouse at Wheeling, Ohio County, (Concluded on page 217)

Deed of the Wetzel Heirs to Frederick Tague

This indenture, made this sixth day of July, 1795, between Frederick Tague of Washington County and State of Pennsylvania of one part, and Mary Wetzel, wife of John Wetzel, deceased, and Martin Wetzel, Lewis Wetzel, Jacob Wetzel, and John Wetzel, Jr., Nathan Guttery and Lucy, his wife, heirs at law of the said John Wetzel, deceased, of the other part.

Witnesseth that the said Mary, Martin, Lewis, Jacob, and John Wetzel, Jr., and Nathan Guttery and Lucy, his wife, for and in consideration of 100 pounds to them in hand paid by the said Frederick Tague, have bargained and sold and by these presents do grant, bargain, sell and convey unto the said Frederick Tague a certain tract or parcel of land lying in Ohio County and State of Virginia containing 400 acres. Being part of a tract of 500 acres formerly granted by Edmund Randolph, Governor of Virginia to John Wetzel by a patent bearing date the thirteenth of June, Anno Domini 1788, and bounded as followeth:

Beginning at a sugar tree on the bank of Big Wheeling Creek by the mouth of a drain. Thence South 140 poles to two white oaks. Thence South 70 degrees; East 180 poles to a white oak. Thence South 71 degrees; East 118 poles to a black oak. Thence North 72 degrees; East 80 poles to a Spanish oak; North 15 degrees; East 170 poles crossing Wheeling Creek to a sugar tree; North 75 degrees; West 80 poles to a hickory; North 43 degrees; West 80 poles to a sycamore on the bank of the creek. Thence down the SEAVOURAL CORSES and meanders thereof 132 poles to a sugar tree and from thence a straight line to the begin-

---

West Virginia. The traps mentioned must have been wolf traps as records show that Captain John Wetzel received 7 shillings and 6 pence from Ohio County, Virginia, on May 3, 1784, for one wolf head.

Colonel David Shepherd received on the same day 3 pounds for 4 wolf heads. Moses Shepherd received on the same day 1 pound, 10 shillings for 1 wolf head; Andrew Zane, 2 pounds, 5 shillings for 3 wolf heads; Elizabeth Tomlinson, 7 shillings, 6 pence for 1 wolf head.

ning with the appurtenances to have and to hold said tract
of land with all its appurtenances to him the said Frederick
Tague, his heirs and assigns forever and the said Mary,
Martin, Lewis, Jacob, and John Wetzel and the said Nathan
Guttery and Lucy, his wife, do covenant to warrant and
defend Frederick Tague, his heirs and assigns, the said
tract each for his or her respective part to Frederick Tague
forever.

In testimony whereof they have hereunto set their hands
and seals the day and date aforesaid.

Mary   ^{her} X _{mark}   Wetzel   [SEAL]

Martin   ^{his} X _{mark}   Wetzel   [SEAL]

Jacob   ^{his} X _{mark}   Wetzel   [SEAL]

John   ^{his} X _{mark}   Wetzel   [SEAL]

Nathan   ^{his} X _{mark}   Guttery   [SEAL]

(Susannah) Lucy ^{her} X _{mark} Guttery [123-124]   [SEAL]

---

123. Signed and acknowledged in open court and recorded in
Deed Book 3, page 144, Ohio County records in the Clerk of the County
Court's office in the Courthouse at Wheeling, W. Va.

124. The name Tague is now changed to Dague. Guttery was
later changed to Goodrich thus Nathan Guttery and Nathan Goodrich is the same person, his wife was mostly known as Susannah
Wetzel. Hence the Lucy Wetzel mentioned in this deed was Susannah
mentioned many times in this book.

Lewis Wetzel was away on a hunting trip and could not be
found to sign this deed. We do not know why Christiana was not
mentioned in the deed.

Deed of Martin Wetzel to Jacob Whetzal

This indenture made this 6th day of June, 1796, between Martin Whetsel of Ohio County, Virginia, of the one part and Jacob Whetzal of the County and State aforesaid of the other part.

Witnesseth; That the said Martin Whetsel for the sum of one thousand dollars doth convey and sell unto the said Jacob Whetzal, his heirs and assigns, the following property, to-wit:

Beginning at a sugar tree and hickory on the bank of a run, and running West 340 poles to a black oak; thence South 470 poles to a white oak; thence East 340 poles to a black oak and chestnut; thence North 470 poles to the beginning, containing one thousand acres of land, being the same tract conveyed to John Whetsell by the said Commonwealth of Virginia by a patent dated June 13, 1788, signed by Edmund Randolph as Governor of Virginia and from his descended to the said Martin Whetsell with its appurtenances to have and to hold the above described tract or parcel of land with its appurtenances to him by Lewis Wetzel and his heirs and assigns forever. In testimony the said Martin Whetsell set his hand and seal this 6th day of June, 1796.

his
Martin X Whetsell [125]   [SEAL]
mark

Deed of Jacob and Rhuhima Wetzel to Robert McConnell

This indenture made this 7th day of June, 1796, by Jacob Wetzel and Rhuhima Wetzel, his wife, of Ohio County, Virginia, of one part and Robert McConnell of Tennessee County, Northwest Territory, of the other part.

Witnesseth: That the said Jacob Wetzel and Rhuhima Wetzel, his wife, for the sum of seven hundred and twenty

125. Recorded in Deed Book 3, Page 301, Ohio County Records in the Courthouse at Wheeling, West Virginia.

dollars cash in hand doth convey and sell unto the said Robert McConnell seven hundred acres of land as follows:

Beginning at a hickory and sugar tree on the run bank and running West 240 poles to an oak; thence South 289 poles to a white oak; thence East 170 poles to a chestnut; thence North 289 poles to the beginning, containing seven hundred acres of land. Being the same property conveyed to John Wetzel by the Commonwealth of Virginia by a patent dated June 13, 1788, and to Martin Wetzel by the heirs and wife of John Wetzel and by Martin Whetsell to Jacob Wetzel by deed dated June 6, 1796.

In testimony thereof the said Jacob Wetzel and Rhuhima Wetzel here set their hands and seal this 7th day of June, 1796.

       his
Jacob X Wetzel   [SEAL]
     mark
       her
Rhuhima X Wetzel [126]   [SEAL]
     mark

Martin, Mary and Jacob Wetzel to Abraham Earliwine

This indenture, made this 29th day of January, 1802, between Martin Wetzel and Mary Wetzel, his wife; Jacob Wetzel and Rhuhima Wetzel, his wife, of Ohio County, Virginia, of one part, and Abraham Earliwine of the County and State aforesaid, of the other part.

WITNESSETH that Martin and Mary Wetzel and Jacob and Rhuhima Wetzel for and in consideration of the sum of $100, cash in hand, paid to them by the said Abraham Earliwine, do hereby grant unto the said Abraham Earliwine, his heirs and assigns forever, a tract or parcel of land in Ohio County and bounded and described as follows:

Beginning at a sugar tree on Earliwine Run and South 10 degrees, East 24 poles to a white oak; South 5 degrees,

---

126. Recorded in Deed Book 3, Page 315, Ohio County Records in the courthouse at Wheeling, West Virginia.

West 26 perches to a white oak; South 15 degrees; West 36 perches to a sassafras, South 26 perches to a white oak; South 17 degrees, East 26 perches to an elm; South 37 degrees, West 60 degrees, West 34 poles to an elm; North 65 degrees, West 91 perches to a Spanish oak; North 7 degrees, West 175 perches to a sugar tree, thence East 168 poles to the beginning containing 191.25 acres and 16 perches of land being a part of a 400 acre tract that was granted Martin Wetzel by a patent bearing date of Feb. 13, 1801, under the hand and seal of James Monroe, Governor of the Commonwealth of Virginia, on a presumption warrant No. 2498 and survey bearing the date of Feb. 13, 1787.

The aforesaid Martin and Mary Wetzel and Jacob and Rhuhima Wetzel do hereby agree to warrant and defend Abraham Earliwine and his heirs and assigns the said tract of land each and for his or her respective part to Abraham Earliwine forever.

In testimony whereof they have hereunto set their hands and seals this day and date aforesaid.

his
Martin X Wetzel   [SEAL]
mark

her
Mary X Wetzel   [SEAL]
mark

his
Jacob X Wetzel   [SEAL]
mark

her
Rhuhima X Wetzel [127]   [SEAL]
mark

Deed of Jacob Wetzel to Archibald Woods and Noah Zane

This indenture made this 9th day of November, 1804, between Jacob Wetzel of the County of Ohio and State of

---

127. Asknowledged in open court, October term, 1806, and recorded in Deed Book 6, Page 132, Ohio County Records, in the Courthouse at Wheeling, West Virginia.

Virginia, of one part, and Archibald Woods and Noah Zane
of the County and State aforesaid, of the other part.
Whereas James Caldwell, Coroner of Ohio County, did on
the 8th day of November, 1804, by virtue of a writ for a
FUCIUS YOUED from the General Court on the 9th day
of July expose to public sale a certain tract of land of 400
acres. The property of the said Jacob Wetzel of which
the said Archibald Woods and Noah Zane being the best
bidders became the purchasers for $800.00, of which tract
the said James Caldwell, Coroner aforesaid, hath executed
a deed in fee simple to the said Archibald Woods and Noah
Zane bearing even date herewith as by reference of the
said deed which will appear more fully as follows:

WITNESSETH that the said Jacob Wetzel in order to
confirm with and establish the title to the said 400 acres of
land aforesaid acquired by Archibald Woods and Noah Zane
for and in consideration of one dollar to him in hand, paid
by the said Archibald Woods and Noah Zane before enseal-
ing and delivering of these presents, the receipt of which
is hereby acknowledged, both granted, sold and conveyed
unto the said Archibald Woods and Noah Zane the following tract of land on Wheeling Creek and Wetzel's Run being
the same tract of land Jacob Wetzel now lives on.

Beginning at a sugar tree on the south side of Wheeling
Creek and Wetzels Run, South 140 poles to a white oak;
thence South 70 degrees, East 180 poles to a Spanish oak;
thence South 71 degrees, East 118 poles to a hickory;
thence North 72 degrees, East 80 poles to a red oak; thence
North 15 degrees, East 170 poles to a white oak, North 75
degrees, West 80 poles to a Gum; thence North 43 degrees,
West 80 poles to a sycamore and from there 143 poles to
the beginning with the appurtenances to have and to hold
said tract of land with all its appurtenances to them the
said Archibald Woods and Noah Zane.

In witnesseth thereof the said Jacob Wetzel has set his hand and seal this 9th day of November, 1804.

his
Jacob X Wetzel   [SEAL]
mark

Witnesseth:
Sealed, signed and delivered in the presence of:
Noah Lindsley,
John Eoff,
Ebenezer Martin.[128]

JOHN, MARTIN AND JACOB WETZEL WERE REAL ESTATE DEALERS AS WELL AS INDIAN FIGHTERS

According to Ohio County records, Martin and Jacob Wetzel and Captain John Wetzel, their father, were real estate dealers as well as Indian fighters.

The following tracts were mostly acquired by Captain John Wetzel, the father of Martin, Lewis, Jacob, John, Jr., George, Susan, and Christiana Wetzel and at the death of Captain John and his son George the land fell to the heirs, who were his wife, Mary Bonnett Wetzel, and her six living children.

Lewis deeded all his rights, title, and interest in the land of his father to his brothers, Martin and Jacob, shouldered his rifle and set out to hunt Indians. John, Jr., deeded his right, title, and interest in most of his father's lands to his brothers Martin and Jacob Wetzel. Jacob lost all his lands and personal property in Ohio County, Virginia.

The following deed of John Wetzel, Jr., and Eleanor Wetzel, his wife, is on record in Deed Book 6 at page 429, Ohio County Records. He bought a tract of land from Moses Shepherd and failing in paying for it, he deeded his

---

128. Recorded in Deed Book 5, Page 518, Ohio County Records, in the Courthouse at Wheeling, West Virginia.

personal property to Moses Shepherd as a part payment on it as follows:

KNOW ALL MEN BY THESE PRESENTS, That I, John Wetzel, of Ohio County, State of Virginia, have this Thirty-first day of October, 1808, bargained, sold and delivered unto Moses Shepherd, Esquire, of the aforesaid County and State all and every piece of property and articles of property which are hereafter mentioned and for the price mentioned in this bill as follows:

For and in consideration and to be part payment of a tract or parcel of land unto the said Moses Shepherd bought by me, the said John Wetzel of the said Moses Shepherd, Esquire, and delivered unto the said Moses Shepherd as part payment for the said tract or parcel of land aforesaid as follows: Viz:

One roan mare, 8 years old	$30.00
One chestnut sorrel mare, 15 yrs.	30.00
One bay horse colt, 2 years old	20.00
One black colt, 2 years old	18.00
One sorrel mare colt, 2 years old	18.00
One black cow about 8 years old	18.00
One red cow, about 7 years old	16.00
One pied cow, about 4 years old	12.00
One brown steer, about 3 years old	6.00
One pied heifer, about 1 year old	3.00
One pied bull, 2 years old	2.00
One red heifer, 3 years old	3.00
One pied heifer calf	1.50
One black heifer calf	1.50
One pied heifer calf	.50

Amount of horses and cows	$179.50
Four spayed sows, 2 years old	$12.00
Two breeding sows, 2 years old	4.00
Seven shoats	7.00

Total Amount	$202.50

One loom and jenny ....$ 8.00
One feather bed, clothes and bedstead...... 20.00
One feather bed, clothes and bedstead...... 8.00
One feather bed, clothes and bedstead...... 8.00
One Chrot[129] 3.00
One driper, furniture, pewter and all........ 5.00
Four sugar kettles,
    one 18 gal., two 10 gal., one 8 gal.......... 8.00
One bake oven, one skillet, two pots........... 4.00
One tea kettle and frying pans................. 2.00
One spinning wheel................................... 1.00
One rifle gun... 8.00
One plow and gears for two horses........... 8.00
One log chain... 2.00

    Total Amount $287.50
Five sheep and two lambs............................$ 7.00
Six acres of corn more or less, in the field
    to be pulled and husked........................... 45.00
The flax of one acre................................... 8.00

TOTAL AMOUNT OF ALL....................................$347.50

All and every piece of the aforesaid articles of property according to their respective prices, I do hereto by these presents accord to this bill deliver unto the aforesaid Moses Shepherd for his use and as his real estate property. I, the said John Wetzel, do bind myself, my heirs, executors, administrators, and assigns, forever to warrant and defend the aforesaid property as the real property of the aforesaid Moses Shepherd and his heirs forever as a part payment from me, the aforesaid John Wetzel, unto the aforesaid Moses Shepherd, for the aforesaid tract or parcel of land bought by me, the aforesaid John Wetzel of the aforesaid Moses Shepherd.

129. This was a German harp something like a bass viol. They got the idea of making a violin from the chrot.

In testimony whereof, I have set my hand and seal this day and date above mentioned.

In presence of me:

his
Nathan X Goodrich
mark

In presence of
George Wetzel

his
John X Wetzel
mark

Eleanor Wetzel [130-131]

---

130.   A true copy from the original which was acknowledged in court at the May term of 1809 by John Wetzel, a party thereto and ordered to be recorded.

Teste; Moses Chapline,
Clerk of the Court.

131.   This property also went to help pay Jacob Wetzel's debts. Other deeds found in the Ohio County Records are as follows:

Deed Book 4, page 75, shows that Martin Wetzel sold 1,000 acres of land to Jacob Wetzel on July 3, 1797, for 100 pounds. The land being on Wheeling Creek.

Deed Book 4, page 267, shows that George Rynehart sold to Martin Wetzel a 100 acre tract of land for 100 pounds.

Deed Book 4, page 69, shows that Mary and Martin Wetzel sold 51 acres of land on July 3, 1797 to Abraham Mercer for 26 pounds and 10 shillings. Colonel George Beeler, George Mercer, and John Mercer were the witnesses.

Also see pp. 239-240, Deed Book 4.

Deed Book 4, Page 82, shows that Sept. 1, 1797, Jacob Wetzel sold to Zephaniah Burch, 100 acres of land on Wheeling Creek for $100.

Deed Book 4, Page 179, shows that Jacob Wetzel sold 200 acres of land on Wheeling Creek to Dennis Brogan on June 4, 1798 for $500.

Deed Book 5, Page 65, shows that Mary and Martin Wetzel sold 191 plus acres of land on Jan. 29, 1802, to Abraham Earliwine for $100.

Deed Book 5, Page 66, shows that Mary and Martin Wetzel sold 100 acres of land on Jan. 1, 1802, to George Walters for $100.

Deed Book 5, Page 154, shows that Mary and Martin Wetzel sold 114 acres of land to John Stewart on Jan. 29, 1802, for $100.

Deed Book 5, Page 180, shows that Mary and Martin Wetzel sold 400 acres of land at the mouth of Stull's Run on Dec. 1, 1802, to James Ewing for $336.65.

Deed Book 5, Page 186, shows that Jacob and Rhuhima Wetzel sold 113 acres of land on Nov. 2, 1802, to Abisha Blodgett for $113.

Deed Book 5, Page 220, shows that Jacob and Rhuhima Wetzel sold 122 acres of land on April 4, 1803, to George Tush for $152.

Deed Book 5, Page 449, shows that Mary and Martin Wetzel sold to Henry Winters, 301 acres of land on Jan. 5, 1805, for $300.

Deed Book 5, Page 450, shows that Mary and Martin Wetzel sold to Jacob Crow on Jan. 5, 1805, 100 acres of land for $100.

Deed Book 5, Page 459, shows that Jacob Wetzel sold 100 acres

Nathan Goodrich to John Wetzel

This indenture made this 31st day of August, 1809, between Nathan Goodrich and Susan, his wife, of the State of Ohio of one part, and John Wetzel of the State of Virginia, County of Ohio, of the other part.

WITNESSETH that for the sum of $240 two hundred and forty dollars in hand, paid by the said John Wetzel to the said Nathan Goodrich and Susan, his wife, they will grant and convey unto the said John Wetzel and his heirs and assigns the following property, to-wit: A certain Tract of land lying on the waters of Wheeling Creek which Tract or Parcel of land was granted to Jacob Wetzel by the Commonwealth of Virginia for 384 acres of land by a patent bearing date of June 4, 1802.

This part of said Tract or Parcel of land containing 100¾ acres was granted by deed of sale by the said Jacob Wetzel and Rhuhima, his wife, to the said Nathan Goodrich and is bounded and described as follows: Beginning at a sugar tree, corner to Moses Shepherd: Thence South 33 degrees, East 100 poles to a maple tree; thence West 122 poles to a red oak; thence South 4 degrees, East 38 poles to a sugar tree; North 57 degrees, West 67 poles to a sugar tree; North 132 poles to a red oak; thence South 68 degrees, East

of land to Nathan Goodrich on Jan. 29, 1805, for $100.

Deed Book 5, Page 461, shows that Jacob Wetzel sold 110 acres of land on Jan. 29, 1805, to John Hisey for $100.

Deed Book 6, Page 175, shows that Mary and Martin Wetzel sold 100 acres of land on Wheeling Creek on July 5, 1806, to Henry Conkle for $30.

Deed Book 6, Page 204, shows that Mary, Martin, Jacob and Rhuhima Wetzel sold 191 acres of land on Earliwine Run on July 5, 1806, to Abraham Earliwine for $30.

Deed Book 6, Page 350, shows that Mary and Martin Wetzel sold 10 acres on Wheeling Creek to Henry Conkle on Sept. 1, 1808, for $10.

Deed Book 7, Page 289, shows that Martin Wetzel sold to Henry Winters, 115 acres of land, April 7, 1812, for $150. This was part of the 500 acres lying near Turkey Run and Viola that was conveyed to John Wetzel June 23, 1783.

Deed Book 20, Page 101, shows that George Wetzel and Priscilla, his wife, sold to his brother-in-law, Alexander Caldwell, his interest in 350 acres of land on Jan. 27, 1835, for $150.

17 poles to the place of beginning containing 100¾ acres
with all its appurtenances unto him the said John Wetzel,
his heirs and assigns forever, and the said Nathan Goodrich
and Susan, his wife, themselves, their heirs and assigns forever, and executors or administrators of the aforesaid lands
with all its appurtenances unto the said John Wetzel, his
heirs and assigns defend from all persons claiming to claim
the land aforesaid.   Witness our hands and seals the day
and date aforesaid.

Nathan Goodrich   [SEAL]

Susan her X Goodrich   [SEAL]
mark

Signed as Witnesses by:
John Caldwell,
Abraham Earliwine,
George Wetzel,
John Siburt.[132]

Deed of Martin Wetzel to Ezekiel Caldwell and John Wetzel

This indenture, made this 11th day of January, 1821,
between Martin Wetzel of Ohio County and State of Virginia of one part, and Ezekiel Caldwell, the son-in-law, and
John Wetzel, the son of the said Martin Wetzel, of the
other part.

Witnesseth that whereas the said Martin Wetzel, being
aged and infirm and desirous of securing to himself and
wife maintenance and support and to pay Andrew Woods a
debt of $150.00 and to provide for his children hereinafter
named in consideration of the premises and in further consideration of the sum of one dollar to him in hand paid by

132.   Proven in open court by the above witnesses and Admitted
to Record February, 1810, in the Clerk of the County Court's Office
in the Courthouse at Wheeling, West Virginia, in Deed Book 7, p. 53.

the said Ezekiel Caldwell and John Wetzel both granted, bargained and sold and by these presents doth grant, bargain and sell unto the said Ezekiel Caldwell and John Wetzel their heirs and assigns forever the following property to-wit: A Tract and Parcel of land whereon the said Martin Wetzel now lives which was granted to him the said Martin Wetzel by a patent bearing date of May 3, 1787, and bounded as follows to-wit: Beginning at a honey locust and white walnut on the banks of Wetzel's Run thence North 39 degrees, West 185 poles to a sugar tree and white walnut on the banks of Wheeling Creek at the mouth of said run. Beginning at the corner of Wetzel's settlement survey; thence crossing said creek North 27 degrees East 200 poles to a black oak; thence North 87 degrees, West 120 poles to a black oak; corner to Abraham Mercer's line, thence with his line South 8 degrees 558 poles to a hickory; thence South 50 degrees; West 60 poles to a sugar tree; thence South 38 degrees, West 20 poles to a hickory; thence South 60 degrees, West 60 degrees to a large white oak; South 3 degrees, West 80 poles and crossing said creek back to a sugar tree, thence leaving Mercer's line South 50 degrees, East 72 poles to a white oak; thence South 23 degrees, East 92 poles to a white oak; thence North 87 degrees, East 212 poles to the beginning, containing 350 acres of land. Also one sorrel mare, 7 years old; one dark bay mare, 8 years old; one bay mare, 13 years old; one black horse, 3 years old; two milch cows; ten head young cattle; all his stock of hogs, and sheep; all his household furniture, consisting of beds, blankets, and other bedding, table and kitchen furniture.

All the wheat and rye now growing on the aforesaid land in the culture of Martin Wetzel. All his farm utensils, plows, barrows, etc. All other personal effects of said Martin Wetzel to have and to hold the Tract aforesaid with all the improvements and appurtenances thereof and hereunto belonging to the said Martin Wetzel. Also all the personal property aforesaid is hereby granted and conveyed unto the

said Ezekiel Caldwell and John Wetzel and their heirs and
assigns forever.   In trust nevertheless and upon the condi-
tion that is to say; that the said Ezekiel Caldwell and John
Wetzel shall out of the rents and profits of the said Tract
of land maintain and support the said Martin Wetzel and
Mary Wetzel, his wife, during their natural lives and at
their decease sell the same for a suitable price and on suitable terms as they or the survivors of them or their administrators or executors shall deem just and right and the
money to be divided equally among all the children of the
said Martin and Mary Wetzel, to-wit; viz. Sarah, George,
Clarissa, Barbara, Mary, Peggy, John, Lewis, Rhoda, and
Ruth or their heirs and the personal effects aforesaid to be
sold by the said Ezekiel Caldwell and John Wetzel and the
proceeds to be applied in discharge of the debt I owe Andrew Woods aforesaid which consists of $150.00 or there-
about, with interest.   The surplus, if any, to be applied on
and of the rents and profits of the said Tract of land aforesaid; should those not be sufficient for the purpose aforesaid.

In witness whereof I have set my hand and seal this day
and date aforesaid.

his
Martin   X   Wetzel,   [SEAL]
mark

her
Mary X Wetzel [133]   [SEAL]
mark

Will of Lewis Bonnett

In the name of God, Amen! I, Lewis Bonnett, of the
County of Ohio and State of Virginia, a farmer being very

---

133.   Acknowledged in open court this 11th day of January, 1821,
by Martin Wetzel and Mary Wetzel, his wife, and Recorded in Deed
Book 10, Page 406, Ohio County Records, in the Courthouse at
Wheeling, West Virginia.

sick and weak in body but of perfect mind and memory,
Thanks be given unto God, calling unto the mortality of
my body, and knowing that it is appointed for all men
once to die, do make and ordain this my last will and testament, that is to say, principally and first of all, I give and
recommend, my soul unto the hand of Almighty God, that
gave it: and my body I recommend to the earth to be buried
in a decent Christian burial, at the discretion of my Executors, nothing doubting but at the General Resurrection I
shall receive the same again by the mighty power of God.
And as touching such worldly estate wherewith it has
pleased God to bless me in this life I give, demise and dis-
pose of the same in the following manner and form.

First: I give and bequeath to my beloved wife Elizabeth
one of my horses creatures, whichever she shall choose and
her side saddle and bridle. One milk cow of her own
choosing, such choice she may renew yearly out of the
stocks which I intend to give my son, John. Also her bed
and bedding, table, and one chest together with the one-
third of all my personal estate as also her living in the
house wherein we now live, and a full third of the part of
the land given to my son, John, that is the benefits there-
from arising during her natural lifetime or so long as she
shall remain my widow and no longer.

Second: I give and devise unto my son Lewis Bonnett
all the upper part of the land that was laid off to him as
will appear by plot bearing date the 26th of November,
1807, to have and to hold to him, after my decease his heirs
and assigns forever, free and clear of all manner of in-
cumbrance whatsoever.

Third: I give and devise unto my son John Bonnett all
the rest or remainder of my plantation for him to have and
to hold to him the said John Bonnett and his heirs and assigns forever, subject still to the third bequeathed to his
mother as is hereinbefore mentioned and paying thereunto
the sum of $415, to be paid in the manner following, that
is to say to my daughter, Mary, who is married to Philip

Rodeffer, $100, to be paid as hereinafter described which, with $100 already received, shall be in full her portion. To my daughter, Barbara, who is married to John Rodeffer, $100, one year after my decease. To Elizabeth Launtz $115, which, together with $85 already paid her, shall be her full portion. To my grandson, Lewis Hooks, I give and bequeath one horse creature worth $50, to be given him by my son John Bonnett as soon as the said Lewis Hooks shall arrive at the age of 21 years.

Further I will direct that one year after my decease my son John Bonnett shall pay as follows to Barbara as is before directed. Next, I direct he shall pay $15 to my daughter, Elizabeth Lantz, which will make her equal with the rest. Then I direct that my son John Bonnett shall two years after my decease to pay $100 every year so as to pay up the $415, and it shall be equally divided among my daughters, Barbara and Elizabeth and Mary, so as their shares shall be equal.

Further, I give and bequeath to my son John Bonnett all the movable property which is not already heretofore mentioned. I further constitutes and appoint my two sons, Lewis Bonnett and John Bonnett my Executors of this, my last will and testament. I hereby revoke and make null and void all and every former wills by me heretofore made, ratifying and confirming this to be my last will and testament and none other.

Witness my hand and seal this 27th day of November, A. D. 1807.

Lewis Bonnett   [SEAL]

Signed, sealed and pronounced as his last will and testament in the presence of us.

John Harner, Donald Keefer, Jesse Burch.[134-135-136]

---

134. Recorded in Will Book 1, Page 13, Ohio County, W. Va., Records. Found in the County Clerk's Office, in the Courthouse at Wheeling, W. Va.

135. Will of John Bonnett: Will Book No. 2, Page 8, in the

Marriage Licenses Issued in Marshall County to the Wetzels

Lewis Wetzel and Eliza Wilkinson. Married January 15, 1850, by Edward Dowler.

Lewis Wetzel and Sarah Coffield. Married April 2, 1850, by James W. Kennan.

James Wetzel, age 24, and Eliza Purdy, age 27. Married November 5, 1868, by George Pelley. James Wetzel was the son of Jeremiah and Lydia Wetzel.

George Alex. Wetzel, age 21, and Elizabeth J. West, age 16. Married July 7, 1875, by Abraham Richmond.

James A. Wetzel, age 20, and Lear R. Anderson, age 24. Married November 11, 1876, by Joseph Anderson.

The following deeds are found on record in the Office of the Clerk of the County Court of Marshall County in the Courthouse at Moundsville, West Virginia.[137]

Courthouse at Wheeling, West Virginia, shows that John Bonnett's will was probated June 21, 1816, and the following heirs were included in the will: Eve, Benjamin, Elizabeth, Simon, and Lewis. John Bonnett died in 1816, aged 81 years, being born in 1735.

136. Will Book No. 1, Page 8, shows the will of Thomas Mc-Creary that was probated August 23, 1802, including: Margaret William, Thomas, Jane and Elizabeth McCreary and Mary Dunlap. Witnesses were Jacob Wetzel and Frans Dodd.

137. Deed Book 2, page 582, shows that Mary Wetzel sold her one-tenth interest in 350 acres of land, on Sept. 19, 1839, for $500 to her brother-in-law, Alexander Caldwell. This was the same land conveyed to Martin Wetzel according to a survey, dated July 26, 1785, and patented to said Martin Wetzel by Beverly Randolph, Lieutenant Governor of Virginia on May 3, 1787.

Deed Book 9, page 182, shows that Barbary Wetzel sold her one-tenth interest in the same 350 acres to Alexander Caldwell on Sept. 15, 1853, for $500.

Deed Book 10, page 56, shows that John Wetzel and Elizabeth Wetzel, his wife, sold their one-tenth interest in the same 350 acres to Alexander Caldwell on July 26, 1854, for $500.

Deed Book 12, page 55, shows that Lewis Wetzel and Margaret, his wife, sold 95 acres of land at the mouth of Burch Run on Oct. 25, 1856, to William Remke for $2,800. This was the original homestead of the Wetzel's now owned by E. J. Wilson.

Deed Book 14, page 111, shows that Lewis Wetzel and Sarah, his wife, who was the wife and widow of Adam Coffield, deceased, and Jacob Coffield, William Coffield, Margaret Coffield, Susanna Coffield, and Joseph Coffield, sold to Thomas McCreary on Sept. 28, 1861, 124 acres of land on Wheeling Creek for $71.87.

Deed Book 19, page 128, shows that Lewis Wetzel and Sarah

Wetzel, his wife, Joseph Coffield, William Coffield, William Clayton, Margaret Clayton, Abraham Coffield, Sarah J. Coffield, George Echols, Elizabeth Echols, George Coffield, Isabella Coffield, Thomas Dowler, John Coffield, and Eliza Coffield, sold to William Coffield 164 acres of land on Nov. 16, 1869, for $810.

Deed Book 24, page 297, shows that Hiram Wetzel and Rosa Wetzel, his wife, of the state of Missouri, sold to Martin Wetzel 94 acres of land in Webster district, on Feb. 16, 1880, for $225.

Deed Book 24, page 328, shows that John T. Wetzel and Mary Wetzel, his wife, sold to Martin Wetzel 94½ acres of land in Webster district on May 19, 1880, for $375.

Deed Book 25, page 81, shows that William and Helen Wetzel, his wife, sold their interest in the same tract of land to Martin Wetzel on March 10, 1881, for $375.

Deed Book 11, page 312, shows that Lewis Wetzel and Margaret Wetzel, his wife, sold to Alexander Caldwell 221 acres of land on Oct. 20, 1856, for $500.

Deed Book 14, page 155, shows that Lewis Wetzel and Sarah Wetzel, his wife, Clarissa Coffield, John Coffield, Eliza Coffield, George and Isabella Coffield sold to Thomas McCreary on Nov. 14, 1861, a tract of land on Wheeling Creek.

Deed Book 25, page 82, shows that Eliza Wetzel, wife of Lewis Wetzel, deceased, Mary J. Allman, Elijah Allman, John D. Wetzel, Mary E. Wetzel, George A. Wetzel, Lear R. Wetzel, William J. Wetzel, Alice Wetzel, and Abraham Wetzel (the latter two being minor children and their shares not included), sold to Martin Wetzel their interest in 94½ acres of land in Webster district on March 1, 1881, for $375.

Deed Book 25, page 84, shows that James Wetzel and Eliza Wetzel, his wife, George Crow and Nancy Crow sold their shares in the same tract of land to Martin Wetzel on April 19, 1881, for $375.

Deed Book 25, page 104, shows that Martin and Margaret Wetzel, his wife, sold to James Robinson on April 19, 1881, 36 acres of land for $1,629.80.

Deed Book 25, page 171, shows that Martin and Margaret Wetzel, his wife, sold to George Crow the home place of Lewis Wetzel, deceased, of 51 acres in Webster district, on April 19, 1881, for $2,439.12.

Records at West Virginia University

The following records were formerly found in the courthouse at Wheeling, W. Va., in the offices of the Clerk of the Circuit Court and the Clerk of the County Court of Ohio County, W. Va., but now are found at West Virginia University, Morgantown, W. Va., where they have been taken for safe keeping and proper indexing.

1802, Jacob Whitzell (Wetzel), Collector of County Levies—Bond.
1802, Jacob Wetzel, Sheriff—Four Bonds.
1803, Margaret Wetzel, Administratrix of John Wetzel, Deceased, Versus, Robert Woods, Administrator of Andrew Robinson, Deceased, Capias.
1804, Jacob Wetzel and Martin Whetzel, Order to view and lay out a road on Wheeling Creek. Viewers Report.
1804, Jacob Whetzel, Allowances for various duties performed.
1804, Martin Wetzel, Overseer—Court Order.
1805, Robert Whetzel, Deceased—Order of appointment of appraisers.
1805, David Williamson, Versus, John Wetzel—Ejectment.
1806, Martin Wetzel, Surveyor—Order to call men to work on road.
1807, Commonwealth, Versus, Martin Wetzel—Indictment for Non-feasance.
1807, Commonwealth, Versus, Martin Whetzell—Two Summons.
1807, Commonwealth, Versus, Martin Wetzel—Assault, Indictment, Summons.
1808, John Whetzel, Versus, Jacob Sailor—Trespass with force of arms.
1808 Commonwealth, Versus, Jacob Wetzel—Assault and Battery.
1808, John Denn, et al Versus, Jacob Wetzel—Ejectment.
1808, James Caldwell, Versus, Jacob Wetzel et al—Breach of Covenant.
1809, Jacob Wetzel, Versus, Nathan Guthridge (goodrich) and John Wetzel—Injunction to restrain payment of money.
1809-1812, Jacob Wetzel and Martin Wetzel—Three Chancery Injunctions.
1819, Commonwealth, Versus, Martin Wetzel—Non-feasance, Indictment and Summons.
1805-1827, Martin Wetzel, Jacob and Rhuhama Wetzel, his wife, and Adam Coffield, 11 miscellaneous damage cases.
1821, Robert Stewart, et al, Versus, Martin Wetzel—Breach of Covenant.
1803-1834, Martin Wetzel, Jacob Wetzel, and George Wetzel—18 Debt Cases.
1806, George W. Gibbon, Versus, Jacob Wetzel—Replevin.
1817, Martin Wetzel, Supervisor of Roads—Order of Appointment.
1830, John Wetel, et al, Overseers of Roads—Order of Appointment.
1830, Lewis Whetzell, Overseer—Order of Appointment.
1852, Conrad Wetzel et al,—Naturalization.

1860, Theodore Wetzel, et al,—Naturalization.

1857-1883, Jacob and John Wetzel—Seven Debt Cases.

1858, J. Wetzel and William Stamm, Keepers of Ordinary-License fee Receipt.

1859, George Reymann and Joseph Wetzel, Keepers of Ordinary-License fee Receipt, Bond.

1883, Ida Wetzel, Versus, Jacob Bart, Breach of Promise of Marriage.

1867, Lewis A. Wetzel, et al, Versus, Fish Creek Branch Oil Co. —Debt.

1880, City of Wheeling, Versus, Jacob and Mary Wetzel, his wife. —Ad Quod Damnum.

1804, Lewis Bonnet, Surveyor—Order of Appointment.

1808, Lewis Bonnett and John Bonnett, Executors for Lewis Bonnett, Deceased.

1816, Lewis Bonnett, and Benjamin McMechen, Executors for John Bonnett, deceased.

1821, Lewis Bonnett, Guardian for heirs of Devalt Keever, deceased.

1821, Commonwealth, Versus, Lewis Bonnett—Misfeasance.

1823, Lewis Bonnett, Sheriff of Ohio County, Va.—Bond.

1825, Lewis Bonnett, Sheriff of Ohio County, Va.—Account for Material and Work, Settlement.

1833, John Bonnett, Bounty for fox scalps.

1834, John Bonnett, bounty for fox and wolf scalps.

1812, Lewis Bonnett, Militia Recommendations.

1815, Lewis Bonnett, Major of First Battalion—Recommendation for Officers.

1804-1832, Lewis Bonnett and Heirs of John Bonnett, Deceased—Papers regarding roads.

1809-1835, Lewis Bonnett, John Bonnett, and Hiram Bonnett, 21 Debt Cases.

1835, Lewis Bonnett, Jr., Indicted for Assault and Battery.

INDEX